Moving & Learning Across the Curriculum

Moving & Learning Across the Curriculum

315 Activities & Games to Make Learning Fun

Rae Pica

Moving & Learning / University of New Hampshire

Delmar Publishers

I⊤P® an International Thomson Publishing company

Albany • Bonn • Boston • Cincinnati • Detroit • London • Madrid
Melbourne • Mexico City • New York • Pacific Grove • Paris • San Francisco
Singapore • Tokyo • Toronto • Washington

NOTICE TO THE READER

Cover illustration by Dawn Bates

Delmar Staff

Publisher: William Brottmiller
Administrative Editor: Jay Whitney
Associate Editor: Erin O'Connor Traylor

Production Coordinator: Barbara A. Bullock
Art and Design Coordinator: Carol Keohane/Jay Purcell
Editorial Assistant: Mara Berman

COPYRIGHT © 1999
By Delmar Publishers
an International Thomson Publishing Company

The ITP logo is a trademark under license.

Printed in the United States of America

For more information, contact:

Delmar Publishers
3 Columbia Circle, Box 15015
Albany, New York 12212-5015

International Thomson
Publishing—Europe
Berkshire House
168-173 High Holborn
London, WC1V 7AA
England

Thomas Nelson Australia
102 Dodds Street
South Melbourne 3205
Victoria, Australia

Nelson Canada
1120 Birchmount Road
Scarborough, Ontario
Canada, M1K 5G4

International Thomson Editores
Campos Eliseos 385, Piso 7
Col Polanco
11560 Mexico D F Mexico

International Thomson
Publishing GmbH
Konigswinterer Strasse 418
53227 Bonn
Germany

International Thomson
Publishing—Asia
60 Albert Street
#15-01 Albert Complex
Singapore 189969

International Thomson
Publishing—Japan
Hirakawacho Kyowa Building,
3F
2-2-1 Hirakawacho
Chiyoda-ku, Tokyo 102
Japan

1 2 3 4 5 6 7 8 9 10 XXX 04 03 02 01 00 99 98

Library of Congress Cataloging-in-Publication Data

Pica, Rae 1953–
    Moving & learning across the curriculum : 315 activities & games
to make learning fun / Rae Pica.
        p.   cm.
    Includes bibliographical references and index.
    ISBN 0-8273-8537-4
    1. Movement education.   2. Early childhood education—Activity
programs.   3. Interdisciplinary approach in education.   I. Title.
GV452P519   1999
372.86'044—dc21   98-4893
                                                          CIP

Contents

Preface   ix

Section One Art   I

Unit 1 *Spatial Relationships*   2
    Personal Space   3
    You Can Take It With You!   5
    Follow the Leader   7

Unit 2 *Shape and Size*   9
    Mirror, Mirror   10
    I Spy . . .   12
    Show Me . . .   14

Unit 3 *Line*   16
    What's My Line?   17
    Up and Down, Side to Side, and Corner to Corner   19
    Drop Me a Line   21

Unit 4 *Color*   23
    What Am I?   24
    Color Me . . .   26
    Primary Colors   28

Unit 5 *Texture*   30
    Soft and Hard   31
    Smooth and Rough   33
    Feathers and Seashells and Bears, Oh My   35

Section Two Language Arts   37

Unit 6 *Listening*   38
    Listen Up!   39
    Get Into Action   41
    How Many Sounds?   43
    What's That Sound?   45

Unit 7 *Speaking* — 47
What's in a Name? — 48
Tell Me About . . . — 50
Four Voices — 52

Unit 8 *Reading* — 54
Action! — 55
Descriptive Words — 57
Happy Endings — 59

Unit 9 *Writing* — 61
Left to Right — 62
Show Me the Letter . . . — 64
Skywriting — 66

Section Three Mathematics — 69

Unit 10 *Quantitative and Positional Concepts* — 71
The Long and the Short of It — 72
Light and Heavy — 74
One More Time — 76
Me and My Shadow — 78
Over the River and Through the Woods — 80

Unit 11 *Number Awareness and Recognition* — 82
Number Shapes I — 83
Number Shapes II — 85
Invisible Numbers — 87

Unit 12 *Counting* — 89
Blast Off! — 90
How Many Parts? — 92
Oh, the Possibilities — 94

Unit 13 *Basic Geometry* — 96
Line 'Em Up — 97
On the Right Path — 99
Right to the Point — 101
What a Square! — 103

Unit 14 *Simple Computation* — 105
"Roll Over" — 106
Add 'Em and Subtract 'Em — 109
How Many Parts Now? — 111

Section Four Music — 113

Unit 15 *Tempo* — 116
Moving Slow/Moving Fast — 117
Moving Slow/Moving Fast — Again — 119
Slow to Fast and Back Again — 121

Unit 16 *Volume* 123
Moving Softly/Moving Loudly 124
Moving Softly/Moving Loudly — Again 126
Soft to Loud and Back Again 128

Unit 17 *Staccato and Legato* 130
"Pop Goes the Weasel" 131
Statues 133
Bound and Free 135

Unit 18 *Pitch* 137
Do-Re-Mi 138
High and Low 140
Moving High/Moving Low 142

Unit 19 *Mood* 144
In a Mellow Mood 145
What Mood Are You In? 147
In the Mood 149

Unit 20 *Rhythm* 151
Body Rhythm 152
Match the Movement 154
Echo 156
Common Meters 158

Section Five Science

161

Unit 21 *My Body* 162
Simon Says 163
Hands Down 165
Move It! 167
Common Senses 169
A Breath of Fresh Air 171

Unit 22 *Hygiene* 173
Rub-a-Dub-Dub 174
Hair Care 176
A Bite Out of Life 178
Laundry Day 180

Unit 23 *Nutrition* 182
Eat Your Fruits and Veggies 183
Get Ready, Spaghetti! 185
Bread, Bread, Bread 187
The Great Pyramid 189

Unit 24 *Seasons* 191
Autumn 192
Winter 194
Spring 196
Summer 198

Unit 25 *Animals* 200
    My Favorite Animal 201
    Rabbits and 'Roos 203
    Giddy-Up 205
    Creepy-Crawly 207
    Ducks, Cows, Cats, and Dogs 209

Unit 26 *Simple Science* 211
    Floating on Air 212
    May the Force Be with You 214
    It's Electric! 216
    Balancing Act 218
    The Machine 220
    It's Magnetic! 222

Section Six Social Studies 225

Unit 27 *Self-Concept* 226
    "If You're Happy" 227
    Oh, What a Feeling 229
    "Punchinello" 231

Unit 28 *Families and Friends* 233
    This Is My Friend 234
    All in the Family 236
    Palm to Palm 238
    Musical Hoops 240
    It Takes Two 242

Unit 29 *Holidays and Celebrations* 244
    Pass the Present 245
    Light the Candles 247
    Let's Hear It for the USA 249

Unit 30 *Occupations* 251
    "This Is the Way We . . ." 252
    Equal Opportunity 254
    Makin' Music 256
    Keepin' House 258

Unit 31 *Transportation* 260
    "Row, Row, Row Your Boat" 261
    Traffic Lights 263
    All Aboard! 265
    By Air or By Sea 267

References 269

Resources 270

Index 273

Preface

When we think of the words *children* and *movement,* physical development is probably the first benefit to come to mind. We might even associate movement with children's social development. But *cognitive* development? What could physical activity possibly have to do with learning?

Confucius said, "What I hear, I forget. What I see, I remember. What I do, I know." Since then, we've discovered the majority of people are more likely to really *know* what they have a chance to *do.* In fact, the more senses involved in the learning process, the greater the impression it makes and the longer it stays with us (Fauth, 1990).

Consider, too, the following points:

★ Young children learn best by doing — through play, experimentation, exploration, and discovery.

★ The term *the whole child* means children come to us as thinking, feeling, moving human beings who learn through all their senses.

★ Research conducted on learning styles shows children acquire knowledge using different modalities and that individuals possess varying degrees of strength in each of them. About 40 percent of students in K–12 consider themselves tactile or kinesthetic learners (either the sense of touch provides the greatest amount of information or doing and moving stimulate learning) (Flaherty, 1992).

★ Body image influences a child's emotional health, learning ability, and intellectual performance.

★ Children think better when their daily routines include physical activity (Taras, 1992).

★ Hannaford (1995, p.13) tells us "movement activates the neural wiring throughout the body, making the whole body the instrument of learning."

All of this points toward a strong connection between mind and body — between moving and learning. But there's more.

For several years, Corso (1993) conducted research on how body/space awareness transfers to paper/space awareness. For example, Corso found when she asked 3- to 8-year-old children to touch their shoulders, some touched only one shoulder. Similarly, some children, when asked to jump and touch the ceiling, reached with only one hand. When requesting samples of the children's papers, Corso discovered the quadrant of paper not used in writing and coloring is the same quadrant of body space not used. Corso's other findings include the following:

★ Children who can't cross midline tend to focus on the vertical of the paper, sometimes writing or drawing down the vertical center of the page and sometimes changing the pencil to the other hand at the midpoint of the paper.

★ Children who have trouble finding a personal space or who line up too closely to the person in front or back of them usually write their letters in a similar pattern.

★ Children who can't cross midline tend to stop reading at the middle of the page.

★ The omission of gross motor instruction may be especially devastating to children who are predominantly kinesthetic learners.

Hannaford (1995), a neurophysiologist and educator, explains that cross-lateral movements, like creeping and crawling, activate both hemispheres of the brain in a balanced way. Because they involve both eyes, ears, hands, and feet, as well as core muscles on both sides of the body, both hemispheres and all four lobes of the brain are activated. This means cognitive functioning is heightened and learning becomes easier.

In addition, the work of Dr. Howard Gardner (1983), a developmental psychologist at Harvard, has helped us understand that children (all humans, in fact) are intelligent in different ways — that they have different ways of learning and knowing. Gardner contends that intelligence is not a singular entity that can be tested only with paper and pencil. Rather, he says we each possess at least eight major intelligences, to greater or lesser degrees, in various combinations. Based on very strict criteria, Gardner determined these intelligences to be the following:

★ **Linguistic Intelligence.** Individuals strong in linguistic intelligence are "word smart." They may have been early talkers and/or readers as children, and they grow up to be the poets, writers, and public speakers in our society.

★ **Logical/Mathematical Intelligence.** People strong in this intelligence are governed by reasoning. They are the scientists, mathematicians, and engineers among us.

★ **Spatial Intelligence.** Individuals with a strong spatial intelligence understand how things orient in space. They are able to visualize and have a strong sense of direction. They often become architects, artists, and navigators.

★ **Naturalist Intelligence.** This intelligence, the most recent to be identified, is, according to Gardner, built into the human nervous system. It is the intelligence that allows individuals to recognize and discriminate among flora and fauna. Botanists and foresters would be among those with a highly developed naturalist intelligence.

★ **Interpersonal Intelligence.** Interpersonal intelligence allows us to understand and relate well to others. Psychologists and counselors are examples of people strong in interpersonal intelligence.

★ **Intrapersonal Intelligence.** Individuals strong in this intelligence know themselves well — both their strengths and their weaknesses. They are usually self-reliant, independent, and goal-directed. Many entrepreneurs fall into this category.

★ **Musical Intelligence.** A fascination with sound and with the patterns created by sound is indication of a strong musical intelligence. Gardner believes this is the first intelligence to develop and, if fostered, leads to a lifelong affinity for music.

★ **Bodily/Kinesthetic Intelligence.** Individuals strong in this intelligence solve problems or create with their bodies or body parts. Actors, dancers, and athletes possess strength in this intelligence, as do surgeons and craftspeople.

Movement experiences, of course, address the bodily/kinesthetic intelligence, but they also enhance spatial intelligence. Activities requiring children to solve movement problems (for example, finding three ways to balance on four body parts) strengthen both intrapersonal and logical/mathematical intelligences. Because music is often used in conjunction with movement, musical intelligence is further developed. Additionally, cooperative activities foster interpersonal intelligence. Using themes from nature and poetry, stories, and songs to inspire movement can address the naturalist and linguistic intelligences.

Obviously, movement must be an integral part of the young child's life and education. When the movement is combined with learning in other content areas, the result is a powerful "one-two punch." Werner and Burton (1979, pp. 1–2) offer six reasons why physical activity is an effective learning medium:

1. Children more readily attend to the learning task . . . When children are physically active, they tend to be totally involved in the learning experience. This assists them in focusing on the relevant attributes of the learning task and helps prevent their attention from being distracted by extraneous factors.
2. The children are dealing with reality. The facts are tangible. An action-oriented learning task provides direct rather than vicarious experience. The children actually manipulate objects or situations. This enables them to see the facts applied and the principles in operation. They do not just read about the content — they experience it.
3. It is a process approach in which development of the affective domain is a primary concern. Affective development is enhanced because the children must closely attend to the stimulus message and actively respond to it. The movement response is both natural and pleasurable and therefore acts as a positive reinforcer. This promotes development of positive attitudes toward the learning process and the particular content being learned.
4. Action-centered learning helps compensate for some of the sensory deficiencies inherent in sedentary activities in which only cognitive operations are employed. When children are physically active, they receive sensory input from their tactual and kinesthetic senses. This makes learning a multisensory experience in which they are feeling as well as observing.
5. It is results-oriented. Each learning activity culminates in an observable goal having been attained. Thus, the children experience immediate rather than delayed gratification.
6. It provides an incentive for self-directed learning. The learning process is exciting and satisfying. This has a tendency to promote participation in learning activities that are self-initiated.

Additionally, movement activities provide teachers an effective means of evaluation. While the traditional question-and-answer method doesn't always reveal students who've failed to grasp the concept being discussed, movement experiences allow the teacher to immediately detect those students who don't understand (Gilbert, 1977).

In many early childhood programs, teachers are torn between what they know about how young children learn and "preparing children for first-grade academics." But the truth is, young children need to *experience* concepts in order to process them — so movement *does* prepare children for later academics! It also strengthens multiple intelligences, includes those children who are kinesthetic learners, and contributes to learning in those children (who happen to be in the majority) who need to use as many senses as possible!

Hannaford (1995, p. 9) writes, "We have spent years and resources struggling to teach people to learn, and yet the standardized achievement test scores go down and illiteracy rises. Could it be that one of the key elements we've been missing is simply movement?"

About This Book

Typically, the early childhood curriculum consists of six major content areas, in addition to physical education (movement): art, language arts, mathematics, music, science, and social studies. This book, therefore, is divided into six sections — one for each content area. They appear in alphabetical order, so as not to give the impression that one content area is more or less important than another.

Each section is introduced with a brief discussion about the content area and its connection to movement. It's my hope that these introductions will help you look at traditional content areas in a whole new light — not just as subjects to be taught but as *potential* — for exploration and discovery, for new ways to bring enthusiasm to the classroom, and for new ideas that help keep you excited about teaching.

Following the introduction to each content area are the lesson plans. Each offers learning objectives ("What It Teaches"); a list of equipment or props required or suggested ("What You'll Need"); the principal activity ("What to Do"); teaching hints ("How to Ensure Success"); possible extensions, variations, and/or alternatives ("What Else You Can Do"); and examples of how the activity and extensions connect with other content areas ("More Curriculum Connectors"). At the end of each lesson plan is a section entitled "What Else I Did." This section has been left blank to allow you to jot down other ideas you (or the children) had while working with the activities, other "connections" made, or notes regarding what worked and what bears repeating.

The lesson plans are organized around topics falling under the major content area. In the cases of science and social studies, the topics are primarily themes commonly explored in classrooms and child-care centers. Because language arts are comprised of listening, speaking, reading, and writing, the language arts section has been divided into those four topics. The remaining content areas — art, mathematics, and music — are organized according to those concepts suitable for exploration with children ages 4 to 8. For every topic, there are three to six lesson plans, arranged from least to most challenging.

The activities are not entirely original in nature (there's much truth in the old adage that "There's nothing new under the sun"). Rather, several stem from tried and tested activities that have been delighting children for years.

Every effort has been made to require as few props as possible. This serves three purposes: (1) to make it easier for the teacher, (2) to ensure these activities can be a part of *every* program, and (3) to provide opportunities for the children to use their *bodies* as tools for learning. It has always been this author's philosophy that the only absolutely necessary piece of equipment required for movement is the child's body.

Finally, the references and resources at the end of the book provide just that — references and resources should you wish to learn more about movement or its use in the classroom. Resources listed include professional organizations and their publications, other relevant publications, movement and physical education book publishers, sources for ordering recordings, sources for ordering equipment and props, and movement specialists and workshops.

How to Use This Book

All early childhood professionals know movement is important in the young child's life and education. Yet not all early childhood professionals make movement part of the curriculum — primarily because they haven't received in-depth training in this subject. So the idea of incorporating movement into the program may at first seem intimidating.

It doesn't have to be that way; this book shows you how easy it can be — perhaps even that you've been on the right course all along!

The lesson plans are designed to be used with children ages 4 to 8. I have not assigned specific ages to each lesson plan, because they are meant to be explored as the children are *developmentally* ready. I have, however, arranged them in order from least to most challenging within each topic. Also, whenever applicable, the topics within each content area are similarly arranged. Furthermore, you will often find suggestions for making an activity less or more challenging under "How to Ensure Success" and "What Else You Can Do."

You know your children better than anyone else and are, therefore, the best judge of what they are or are not capable of. Trust your judgment. If you try an activity and find your children aren't ready for it, consider it a valuable learning experience — and try it again at a later time.

When exploring a concept with children, simply remember the first part of this introduction — not all children learn in the same way, they possess various intelligences, and more is retained as more senses are employed. So, talk to the children about the concept (this is particularly helpful for auditory learners). Demonstrate for the visual learners. Provide opportunities for tactile learners to touch. For the kinesthetic learners — and *all* children who learn by doing and by using a combination of senses and intelligences — choose an activity from this book that relates to the concept being explored, or let the activities suggested here inspire ideas of your own!

Whenever possible, participation in these games and activities should not be isolated events; that is, they should be connected, as much as possible, to the daily curriculum. For example, the lesson plan calling for exploration of descriptive words (found under "Language Arts") doesn't have to use an arbitrary list of descriptive words. Rather, if you've just read a story to the children consisting of a number of descriptive words, you could then use those words as impetus for the movement activity. As another example, the activities under "Art" can be employed in conjunction with specific art projects — for instance, a project relating to shape or color. The activities within each lesson plan can also be easily excerpted and incorporated into one of your own lesson plans.

Movement makes its greatest impact as a tool for learning when it is used together with other approaches. As with any aspect of early childhood education, young children do not learn best when subjects are segregated. (Content areas are separated in this book to promote both understanding and organization.)

Other occasions when you might refer to this book include:

★ when the children have been sitting too long and need an opportunity to move;

★ when you need a transitional activity;

★ when the children just aren't "getting it" through other teaching methods;

★ when you and/or the children are in need of something new — and fun — to do; and

★ when you want to help parents and others understand why movement is essential to the early childhood curriculum and just how much it has to teach.

Remember — every teacher and every child brings new ideas and new potential to the concept of moving and learning. Use these activities — as well as those they're sure to inspire — to enhance learning, develop rapport among children, gain immediate feedback, promote a positive attitude toward education that can influence future learning, and, above all, to educate the whole child!

Acknowledgments

I'd like to offer my appreciation to the following people for their contributions, both direct and indirect, to this book. Many thanks to:

★ Jay Whitney at Delmar, for his belief in me;

★ my editor, Erin O'Connor Traylor, for her patience, insight, and assistance;

★ my illustrator and friend, Dawn Bates, for being so very good at both those jobs;

★ my friends Sheila Chapman and Patti Page, for their unfaltering love and support;

★ my husband, Richard Gardzina, for the life, laughter, and love we've shared these many years; and

★ my reviewers, for their time, energy, and suggestions.

Julia Beyeler, Ph.D.
University of Akron, Wayne College
Orrville, OH

Betty Culberston
San Antonio College
San Antonio, TX

Toni Cacace-Beshears
Tidewater Community College
Portsmouth, VA

Eilene Glasgow, Ph.D.
Pacific Lutheran University and Seabury School
Tacoma, WA

Rhonda Clements, Ed.D.
Hofstra University
Hempstead, NY

Carol Totsky Hammett
Bend-La Pine Public Schools
Bend, OR

ART

Art ★ Language Arts ★ Mathematics ★ Music ★ Science ★ Social Studies

Art and movement have a number of things in common — particularly where young children are concerned. Art, because it involves movement, helps develop motor skills. Gross motor skills are used in such art activities as painting on an easel, creating murals, body tracing, and working with clay. Fine motor control, which is refined later than gross motor control, is practiced during such art activities as working with small paintbrushes, cutting with scissors, and pasting. Both art and movement also help develop eye-hand coordination (Schirrmacher, 1998; Mayesky, 1998).

But perhaps the most significant common factor between art and movement is that self-expression is encouraged. When given ample opportunity to explore possibilities — whether through movement or a variety of art materials — children make nonverbal statements about who they are and what is important to them. Through both mediums, they can express emotions and work out issues of concern to them and achieve the satisfaction that comes from experiencing success. These results can only occur, however, when the child's movement responses and artwork aren't censored by adults and when they're accepted and valued as evidence of the child's individuality. With such acceptance, children gain confidence in their abilities to express themselves, solve problems, and use their creativity.

Finally, concepts like shape, size, spatial relationships, and line are also part of art and movement education. Thus, whenever children arrange their bodies in the space around them, they're exploring artistic as well as physical concepts. With their bodies, they're creating lines and shapes. When they move into different levels, in different directions, along different pathways, and in relation to others and to objects, they're increasing their spatial awareness. Yet, even such artistic concepts as color and texture can be explored and expressed through movement.

Spatial Relationships

Art ★ Language Arts ★ Mathematics ★ Music ★ Science ★ Social Studies

Personal Space

What It Teaches

★ The concept of personal space

★ Respect for others' personal space

What You'll Need

Carpet squares or hula hoops and "New Age" (preferably nonrhythmic) music (all optional)

What to Do

★ Have each child find a spot to stand in, far enough away from each other so they can stretch out their arms without touching anyone else.

★ Ask them to reach their arms as high, low, and wide as they can without moving from their spots. Challenge them to explore all the space around their bodies. How high can they get? How low? Have they checked out the area in between? What other body parts can they explore with?

★ Explain that they've just explored their very own personal space, and it's very much like being inside a giant bubble!

How to Ensure Success

Some children need tangible evidence of personal space. Provide carpet squares or hoops if you think they'll be helpful. Ask the children to imagine they're each on their own little island.

What Else You Can Do

★ To grant the children even greater ownership of their personal spaces — and to stimulate imaginations — ask the children to pretend to paint the insides of their spaces. They can decorate with stripes or polka dots or with any colors they want.

★ Challenge the children to discover how many ways they can move with their feet "glued" to the floor. After a while, allow them to unglue one foot and, finally, both. (Remind them they must still stay in their personal spaces.)

More Curriculum Connectors

 Self-concept, which is explored through the idea of personal space, is the beginning of **social studies** for young children.

 Ask the children to describe how they've decorated their personal spaces to make **language arts** part of the process.

 Play "New Age" **music** in the background as the children are creating their spaces.

 The positional concepts of high, low, and wide are part of **mathematics**.

What Else I Did

_____

_____

_____

_____

_____

You Can Take It With You!

What It Teaches

★ The concepts of personal and general space

★ Respect for others' space

What You'll Need

One hoop per child, if possible

What to Do

★ Once the children understand the idea of personal space, explain that personal space goes with us wherever we go.

★ If you have enough hoops for everyone, hand them out and ask the children to each step inside one, lifting it to around the waist. (If you don't have hoops, ask the children to reach their arms out to the sides.)

★ Challenge the children to walk all around the room without letting their hoops — or hands — touch anyone else's. Once they're succeeding at this, you can increase the challenge by asking them to vary their speed or to move in backward or sideward directions.

How to Ensure Success

For some children, adding some imagination to the mix heightens the challenge — and therefore the experience. You can ask your group to imagine their hoops (or hands) are electrically charged and they must be very careful not to get shocked!

Begin simply, with the children moving forward, along straight pathways. Wait until they've mastered this before asking them to try other directions as well as curving and zigzag pathways.

What Else You Can Do

★ When your children demonstrate they can respect one another's personal space, they're ready to play Shrinking Room. In this game, you stand with your arms and legs outstretched, pretending to be a wall. Begin at one end of the room, allowing the children the maximum amount of space in which to move without touching one another. Then take a big step forward, decreasing the size of the room (and the space in which they have to move). Continue gradually reducing the size of the room, stopping while the children are still able to succeed.

More Curriculum Connectors

 Respecting the personal space of others constitutes **social studies**.

 Gradual reduction of the size of the room is a lesson in **mathematics**.

What Else I Did

_____

_____

_____

_____

_____

Follow the Leader

What It Teaches

★ The concept of general space

★ Visual discrimination

★ The ability to physically replicate what the eyes see

★ Practice with locomotor skills

What You'll Need

No equipment needed

What to Do

★ Play the traditional game of Follow the Leader, making sure to include lots of variety in levels, pathways, directions, and locomotor skills. For example, you can move on tiptoe or as small as you can be (levels); forward, backward, and sideward (directions); in straight, curving, circular, and zigzagging pathways. You can use any form of locomotion the children can execute successfully (walking, running, galloping, leaping, etc.).

How to Ensure Success

Start off slowly, with the simplest examples for the children to follow.

At first, don't change what you're doing often. Give the children lots of opportunity to master following you before modifying the challenge.

Make sure all the children can see you!

What Else You Can Do

★ When the children are ready for the challenge, you can explore the concepts of *accelerando* (gradual increase in tempo, or speed) and *ritardando* (gradual decrease in speed). Start — and end — with a very slow walk, exploring the full range from very slow to very fast.

★ When the children are developmentally ready to act as leaders, you can modify the game. Begin as usual, but after a few minutes, call out the name of one of the children. That child breaks off from the line, with everybody behind her following her instead of you. Continue to do this until you have several small lines moving throughout the room. Also, occasionally call out "Switch," indicating the child in front of the line should move to the back, creating a new leader.

More Curriculum Connectors

 The cooperation involved in this activity is a lesson in **social studies**.

 Being able to physically replicate what the eyes see is necessary in writing, which is part of **language arts**.

 In the extension activity, you can count the number of children in each of the lines, contributing to knowledge in **mathematics**.

 Accelerando and ritardando are **musical** concepts.

What Else I Did

_____

_____

_____

_____

_____

UNIT 2
Shape and Size

Mirror, Mirror

What It Teaches

★ Shape awareness

★ Visual discrimination

★ Ability to physically replicate what the eyes see

What You'll Need

No equipment needed

What to Do

★ Talk to the children about how mirrors work. Where in their houses do they have mirrors?

★ Explain that you're going to stand in front of them and they should pretend they're your mirror reflection — doing what you do and resembling you as closely as possible.

★ Create various shapes with your body, at different levels in space. Possibilities include round, straight, wide, narrow, and pointed.

How to Ensure Success

At first, move very slowly from one position to another, using as few body parts as possible (for example, just the arms, as opposed to an arm and a leg).

Begin with the simplest shapes. When the children are developmentally ready, you can include more difficult shapes, like crooked, angular, or oval. Also, explore symmetrical shapes before you begin demonstrating asymmetrical ones.

What Else You Can Do

★ When the children no longer need you to demonstrate, simply ask them to show you body shapes that are round, straight, wide, narrow, etc.

★ When the children are ready to cooperate with partners, they can pair off and play a mirror game in twos. Partners take turns initiating and imitating.

More Curriculum Connectors

 The concept of mirror reflection relates to **science**.

 Shape is also part of geometry, which is part of **mathematics**.

Being able to physically replicate what the eyes see is a necessary part of learning to write, which falls under the heading of **language arts**.

Cooperating with a partner constitutes **social studies**.

What Else I Did

_____

_____

_____

_____

_____

I Spy . . .

What It Teaches

★   Shape awareness

★   Visual discrimination

★   Ability to physically replicate what the eyes see

What You'll Need

Objects typically found in a classroom; pictures or actual examples of teapots

What to Do

★   Point out objects of fairly simple shape throughout the room, discussing the various shapes with the children. Possible objects might include a desk, chair, chalkboard, rug, stuffed animal, piece of chalk, piece of paper, etc.

★   Challenge the children to take on the shapes of these objects.

How to Ensure Success

Discuss one object at a time and then ask the children to take on its shape while the description is still fresh in their minds.

Use simple descriptions with the children, like *flat* or *round*, *long* or *short*. Also, it's best to first ask for their descriptions. Then, if they need more direction, you can specifically ask if an object is flat or round, etc.

Refine their responses with follow-up questions and challenges. For example, if a child depicts the roundness of a rug but not the flatness, you might ask if he can get as close to the floor as the rug actually is.

What Else You Can Do

★   Show the children pictures or actual examples of teapots in different shapes and sizes. Then sing "I'm a Little Teapot." Encourage a variety of responses.

★   Chant "I spy with my little eye something in the room that's long and straight (short and round, very crooked, etc.) . . ." The children then look around, determine what it could be, and take on the shape themselves. (It's best if more than one possible response exists to each challenge.) They can then tell you what object they've each chosen to depict.

More Curriculum Connectors

 Shape is also part of geometry, which is part of **mathematics**.

 Being able to physically replicate what the eyes see is a necessary part of learning to write, which constitutes **language arts**, as does describing the shapes. You can also incorporate Dayle Ann Dodds' book, *The Shape of Things,* into your lesson.

 Singing "I'm a Little Teapot" brings **music** into the mix.

What Else I Did

_____

_____

_____

_____

_____

Show Me . . .

What It Teaches

★ Shape and size awareness

★ Comparisons

★ An introduction to suffixes

What You'll Need

No equipment needed

What to Do

★ Ask the children to show you a big shape. Then challenge them to make it a little bigger and, finally, the biggest it can be.

★ Continue with such challenges as *little, littler, littlest; round, rounder, roundest; long, longer, longest;* etc.

How to Ensure Success

At first, it might help if you demonstrate this concept yourself. You could also use objects such as straws to demonstrate the concept.

What Else You Can Do

★ When the children are developmentally ready, divide the class into groups of three. Then challenge each group to illustrate, among themselves, some of the examples listed previously, and others.

More Curriculum Connectors

 Shape and size also relate to **mathematics**, as does the concept of comparison.

 Suffixes fall under the heading of **language arts**. The book *The Best Bug Parade* by Stuart J. Murphy is about size relationships.

 The cooperation required in the extension activity comes under the heading of **social studies**.

What Else I Did

_____

_____

_____

_____

_____

UNIT 3
Line

What's My Line?

What It Teaches

★   The concept of line

★   Visual discrimination

★   Ability to physically replicate what the eyes see

What You'll Need

Drawings or examples of straight, curving, and crooked lines

What to Do

★   Show the children drawings or actual examples of lines that are straight, curving, and crooked. Can they describe what makes a line curving versus crooked?

★   Ask them to show you, with their whole bodies, straight, curving, and crooked lines.

★   Can they find at least two different body parts (e.g., arms, legs, fingers) with which to demonstrate straight, curving, and crooked lines?

How to Ensure Success

Provide as much direct instruction (i.e., demonstration and imitation) as necessary in the beginning.

Suggest *stretching* to ensure straightness and *roundness* to encourage curves. This might also be a good time to introduce the children to the word *angle* in relation to crooked lines.

What Else You Can Do

★   Call out the words *straight, curving,* and *crooked* — at varying tempos and in various orders — challenging the children to match their body shape with the word called.

★   Play Heads, Bellies, Toes, in which you call out these body parts at varying tempos and in varying orders, with the children touching the body part(s)

called. With this version, however, you can add the extra challenge of asking children to assume a straight body line while touching the head, a curving body line while touching the belly, and a crooked body line while touching toes. (You can substitute the word *tummies* for bellies if the children are more familiar with it.)

More Curriculum Connectors

 Line is also part of basic geometry, so it falls under **mathematics**.

 Describing lines constitutes **language arts**.

 Identifying body parts is basic **science**.

What Else I Did

_____

_____

_____

_____

_____

Up and Down, Side to Side, and Corner to Corner

What It Teaches

★ The concept of line

★ Visual discrimination

★ Ability to physically replicate what the eyes see

What You'll Need

A jump rope, or something similar, for demonstration purposes

What to Do

★ Introduce the concepts of *vertical, horizontal,* and *diagonal* by using the jump rope to demonstrate these kinds of lines for the children.

★ As you demonstrate each of the preceding, challenge the children to show you the same kind of line with their bodies and, later, with body parts.

How to Ensure Success

At first, you'll want to provide a constant visual demonstration for the children as they form the various lines with their bodies. In other words, if you're using a jump rope to demonstrate a line, hold it in position until the children have finished creating their shapes. (Later, you can demonstrate briefly and then challenge the children to replicate what they saw.)

What Else You Can Do

★ Once the children have had a lot of experience with these types of lines, you can ask them to show you horizontal, vertical, and diagonal without any visual aids.

★ Ask the children to "paint" imaginary lines of all kinds in the air — first with their hands and then with various other body parts — and on the floor, with their feet. Can they do it with both left and right hands and feet? What colors do they imagine their lines to be?

More Curriculum Connectors

 Line is also part of simple geometry, or **mathematics**.

 Ask the children to identify which letters of the alphabet include horizontal, vertical, and diagonal lines, making **language arts** part of the project.

What Else I Did

_____

_____

_____

_____

_____

Drop Me a Line

What It Teaches

★ The concept of line

★ Visual discrimination

★ Pathways

What You'll Need

Several jump ropes, or masking tape, to create visible pathways; materials for an obstacle course (optional)

What to Do

★ Use jump ropes or masking tape to create a variety of lines on the floor. Be sure to include all lines the children have had experience with to this point (e.g., straight, curving, crooked, horizontal, vertical, and diagonal).

★ Acting as leader, play Follow the Leader with the children, following the pathways created by the rope or tape. Once the children are familiar with this activity, they can take turns acting as leader.

How to Ensure Success

Begin by simply walking along the created pathways. Later, you can try following them with other locomotor (traveling) skills (run, jump, leap, gallop, slide, skip).

Make each pathway as big or long as possible so the children have a chance to fully experience them.

What Else You Can Do

★ Bring the game outside, where there is a possibility of even longer pathways.

★ Explore various elements of movement by leading or encouraging the children to move with different amounts of force (tiptoeing or stomping, for instance), in different body shapes, or at different tempos (slowly and quickly).

★ Make your lines part of an obstacle course that also includes tunnels (old tires and appliance boxes work just fine), objects to crawl and creep over and under, and obstacles to move around. (Obstacle courses are great outside, too.)

More Curriculum Connectors

Line and positional concepts come under the heading of **mathematics**.

Experimenting with different amounts of force falls under the heading of **science**, while tempo belongs to the content area of **music**.

Follow the Leader is a cooperative activity, which makes it **social studies**.

What Else I Did

_____

_____

_____

_____

_____

UNIT 4

Color

What Am I?

What It Teaches

★ Color and shape awareness

What You'll Need

Pictures or examples of objects in various colors

What to Do

★ Show the children pictures or examples of objects in various colors — one at a time — and ask the children to demonstrate the shape of each object. Possibilities include a yellow banana, a green plant, a red apple, an orange, a bunch of purple grapes, or a white snowflake.

How to Ensure Success

Since the idea behind this activity is to associate certain colors with certain shapes, show the children objects that are typically one shape and one color. For example, a *bowl* generally comes in one shape but could be any color. On the other hand, a banana has a particular shape and is most often yellow.

If necessary, provide additional guidance by talking about curves and straight lines, etc. At first, you may want to demonstrate the shapes yourself.

What Else You Can Do

★ Give the children an assortment of objects from which to choose. Then, each child picks one and takes on its shape. Ask the rest of the children to guess which object it is.

★ Play What's Missing? with the objects. With this game, one child hides his eyes as another removes an object and places it behind her back. (All the children place their hands behind their backs so the child guessing doesn't know who took it.) The teacher then instructs the first child to open his eyes and asks him to guess what's missing. In this version, the child guessing should also include the *color* of the object.

★ Use the children's book *Brown Bear, Brown Bear, What Do You See?* (written by Bill Martin, Jr. and illustrated by Eric Carle) to inspire a discussion of differently-colored creatures, both real and imaginary (e.g., a green frog and a purple cat). Then invite the children to show you how some of these creatures *move*.

More Curriculum Connectors

 Identifying and sorting are part of both **mathematics** and **science**.

 The guessing games bring in **language arts**, as does the children's book.

What Else I Did

_____

_____

_____

_____

_____

Color Me . . .

What It Teaches

★ Color discrimination

★ Self-expression

What You'll Need

A variety of colors

What to Do

★ Show the children different colors, one at a time, discussing what each reminds them of. Does the color bring certain objects, or perhaps creatures, to mind? Certain feelings?

★ Again display each color one at a time, asking the children to show you *with their bodies* what the color brings to mind.

How to Ensure Success

Use only colors with which the children are very familiar — and have several possible associations — until they're ready for greater challenges. To begin, possibilities include red, blue, yellow, green, white, and black.

Be sure to validate all responses so the children understand it's possible — and okay — to have different ideas. For example, the color blue could have a wide variety of meanings to the children; it could bring to mind the sky, water, feeling sad, or feeling cold, or it could conjure up an image you would never think of!

What Else You Can Do

★ Assign small groups (of perhaps three children) to represent different colors. When you call out a group's color, those children each demonstrate what it means to them. The rest of the children can try to guess what the different responses represent.

More Curriculum Connectors

 Self-expression is an important part of early **social studies**. You can also incorporate multicultural education with Katie Kissinger's book, *All the Colors We Are: The Story of How We Get Our Skin Color*. (Each page has both Spanish and English.)

 Talking about the colors' associations constitutes **language arts**.

 Counting the number of different responses for each color includes **mathematics**.

What Else I Did

_____

_____

_____

_____

_____

Primary Colors

What It Teaches

★ Color discrimination

★ Primary colors

★ Self-expression

★ Cooperation

What You'll Need

Objects or paint samples in red, yellow, and blue; red, yellow, and blue paint (optional)

What to Do

★ Show the children red, yellow, and blue paint samples — or objects — explaining that these are the three primary colors from which other colors are created.

★ Divide the class into three groups, assigning each a primary color.

★ Challenge the members of each group to think of and demonstrate as many different things in their color as they can.

How to Ensure Success

Actually demonstrating with paints, sheer scarves, color palettes, or cellophane can help the children see how the three primary colors create others. Show them, or let them discover for themselves, what happens when red and yellow, red and blue, and yellow and blue are mixed.

Allow the children to demonstrate their responses, either individually, with others in the group, or with the group as a whole — whatever they find most appropriate. For example, if the color yellow reminds one child of the sun, she might want to act as the center, with the rest of her group surrounding her as the rays, or she might choose to simply "shine" on her own.

What Else You Can Do

★ Once the children understand this concept, you can begin "mixing" them. In other words, assign one child from each group to pair with a child from a different group. Each pair then depicts something in the color they've created with their joining (you can tell them what color it is, if necessary). For instance, if a child from the red group and a child from the blue group form a pair, they must create something purple. You can ask all the pairs to work concurrently, or you can ask one pair at a time for a response, which that pair demonstrates for the rest of the class while the class guesses what the response is.

More Curriculum Connectors

 The self-expression and cooperation required in these activities fall under the heading of **social studies**.

 You and the children can count the number of different responses for each color to incorporate **mathematics**.

 You can include **language arts** by introducing (or reintroducing) the children to Tana Hoban's book *Is It Red? Is It Yellow? Is It Blue?* or Eric Carle's *My First Book of Colors*.

 Include Hap Palmer's "Colors" (from Volume I of *Learning Basic Skills Through Music*) and "Parade of Colors" (from Volume II) to incorporate **music**.

What Else I Did

_____

_____

_____

_____

_____

Texture

Art ★ Language Arts ★ Mathematics ★ Music ★ Science ★ Social Studies

Soft and Hard

What It Teaches

★ Texture awareness

★ Experience with the sense of touch

★ The movement element of force

What You'll Need

A variety of both soft and hard objects (possibilities for soft items include stuffed animals, facial tissue, blankets, swatches of velvet or flannel; hard items might include a rock, key, coin, or marble); loud and soft music (optional); a statue and a rag doll (optional)

What to Do

★ Allow the children to touch all the objects.

★ Ask them to tell you what they think the differences are between hard and soft.

★ Now ask them to demonstrate the difference between hard and soft by moving their bodies and/or body parts.

How to Ensure Success

The children may find it easier at first to perform locomotor (traveling) movements that demonstrate the difference between hard and soft — for example, stamping for hard and tiptoeing for soft. Later, you can ask them to show you with their muscles alone, remaining in one spot (i.e., tightening the muscles for hard and relaxing them for soft).

Using loud and soft music might help make these concepts less abstract; loud music tends to inspire forceful (hard) movements and soft music gentle (soft) movements.

What Else You Can Do

★ Ask the children to think about the difference in texture between a statue and a rag doll (show them both, if possible). Which is harder, and which is softer?

Ask them to show you what they'd look like if they were statues, then rag dolls. Once they can demonstrate the difference in muscle tension, alternately call out the words *statue* and *rag doll*, challenging the children to match the word called with the appropriate body posture. Vary the amount of time between words. (Since this is technically contracting and releasing muscles, you can use this, with the children lying down, as a relaxation exercise. Just be sure to end with the rag doll!)

More Curriculum Connectors

 Exploring the concepts of touch and muscle tension are both **science** activities. The scientific concept of *cause and effect* can also be explored by letting an ice cube or a stick of butter sit out all day. What happens? The children can then demonstrate melting with their bodies.

 Using **music** will add yet another content area.

 Discussing the differences between textures constitutes **language arts**.

What Else I Did

_____

_____

_____

_____

_____

Smooth and Rough

What It Teaches

★ Texture awareness

★ Experience with the sense of touch

★ The movement element of flow

What You'll Need

A variety of both smooth and rough objects (possibilities for smooth items include a marble, mirror, and swatch of satin or plastic; rough objects could include burlap, rope, and sandpaper)

What to Do

★ Allow the children to touch all the objects.

★ Ask the children to tell you what they think the differences are between smooth and rough.

★ Ask them to show you the difference between moving smoothly and moving roughly.

How to Ensure Success

Providing familiar images might help the children understand these concepts better. For example, ice skaters gliding and eagles soaring move smoothly, while wind-up toys and robots move roughly.

What Else You Can Do

★ Increase comprehension of certain descriptive words by calling out a variety of them relative to *smooth* and *rough* and challenging the children to demonstrate their meanings. Possibilities to inspire smooth movement include *lightly, gliding, flowing,* and *floating.* Words that can conjure up rough movement include *jerky, stop-and-go, bumpy,* and *jagged.*

★ Once the children understand the meanings of these words, alternate calling out a "smooth" word with a "rough" one, challenging them to change their movements accordingly.

More Curriculum Connectors

 Exploring the sense of touch involves **science**.

 Discussing the differences between smooth and rough and exploring descriptive words fall under the heading of **language arts**.

What Else I Did

_____

_____

_____

_____

_____

Feathers and Seashells and Bears, Oh My

What It Teaches

★ Awareness of texture

★ Experience with the sense of touch

★ Self-expression

What You'll Need

Items of various textures (for example, rope, burlap, feathers, beach ball, stuffed animal, carpet square, and facial tissue)

What to Do

★ Talk to the children about how each item feels or makes them feel (a feather, for instance, might make them feel ticklish, while burlap makes them itch).

★ Ask the children to demonstrate their responses through movement.

How to Ensure Success

If the children need prompting, you can be more direct with your questions. For example, how would their bodies move if they were feeling ticklish? If they were itchy all over?

What Else You Can Do

★ An alternate activity is to ask the children to move *like* the item exhibited. For example, how does a feather move? A teddy bear? A beach ball?

★ Challenge the children to move all around the room, feeling for different textures. Can they create different sounds and rhythms with these textures? (For instance, a carpet makes a different sound than a chalkboard.) Can they move to the sounds and rhythms they create?

More Curriculum Connectors

 The sense of touch also relates to **science**.

 Self-expression is one of the early stages of **social studies**.

 Music is about creating sounds.

 Discussing how the various items feel constitutes **language arts**. You can also incorporate Karen Bryant Mole's book *Texture* into the exploration of this topic.

What Else I Did

_____

_____

_____

_____

_____

LANGUAGE ARTS

The language arts include the interrelated and overlapping components of listening, speaking, reading, and writing. Therefore, being about communication — imparted or received — this content area plays a vital role in every individual's life. It is also part of every curriculum, in one form or another, from preschool through advanced education. Also, it is tied to linguistic intelligence, which is granted enormous validation in our society.

In early childhood programs, language arts have traditionally received the greatest concentration during daily group or circle times. During these periods, teachers and caregivers read stories or poems to the children, who sit and listen. Sometimes discussion precedes or follows the readings. In elementary schools, reading and writing have all too commonly been handled as separate studies, with the children focusing on topics like phonics, spelling, and grammar.

The whole-language approach to children's emerging literacy recognizes that listening, speaking, reading, and writing overlap and interrelate, each contributing to the growth of the others. This approach also acknowledges that children learn best those concepts that are relevant to them. Therefore, their language acquisition and development must be a natural process that occurs over time, relates to all aspects of the children's lives, and *actively* involves the children in making meaning (Sawyer & Sawyer, 1993; Raines & Canady, 1990).

Movement, like language, plays an essential role in life and is also a form of communication. "Body language," in fact, is a very distinct form of communication. Thus, movement and the language arts are naturally linked. Teachers who adopt a whole-language or integrated approach to literacy soon realize movement is a vital tool in the acquisition and development of the language arts. They also realize there's no end to the number of ways to explore the language arts through movement!

Listening

Listen Up!

What It Teaches

★   Auditory discrimination

★   Memory

What You'll Need

No equipment needed

What to Do

★   Sitting on the floor with the children, tell them you're going to give them three different words, all beginning with the letter *s*, that each have a different action.

★   When they hear you say the word *seal,* they should clap their hands in front of them like a seal. When you say the word *sunshine,* they make a circle with their arms above their heads. When they hear you say the word *salute,* they perform a salute with hand to the forehead.

★   Play the game for as long as the children stay interested, constantly mixing up the order of the words.

How to Ensure Success

Explain that they must listen very carefully, beyond the initial sound of the word, before performing the action. You're not trying to trick them; you want to see how well they can listen!

What Else You Can Do

★   To make the game even more challenging, add some other words beginning with *s,* for which the children are not expected to perform an action. (Possibilities include *sandwich, snowshoe, sink, smile,* and *submarine.*) The extra words mean they'll really have to listen carefully.

★   Play the game with words beginning with other letters.

More Curriculum Connectors

 Sound discrimination is also part of **music**.

 Focusing on the sense of hearing falls under the heading of **science**.

What Else I Did

_____

_____

_____

_____

_____

Get Into Action

What It Teaches

★   Auditory sequential memory

★   Listening skills

What You'll Need

No equipment needed

What to Do

★   Tell the children you're going to give them a list of movements to do but that they're not to start doing them until you've finished speaking.

★   Start with a short sequence, for example, clap twice, blink eyes.

★   As the children are ready, lengthen the sequence, for example, clap twice, blink eyes, turn around (jump in place, sit down, etc.).

How to Ensure Success

Begin by performing the actions with the children as you say the words. When the children are ready, eliminate your actions.

What Else You Can Do

★   Eliminate lines from familiar fingerplays (while still performing the actions) to test the children's memories and listening skills. (Books of fingerplays include *Move Over, Mother Goose* by Ruth Dowell, *Finger Frolics: Fingerplays for Young Children* by Liz Cromwell and Dixie Hibner, *Mitt Magic: Fingerplays for Finger Puppets, Ring a Ring o' Roses* by Flint Public Library, and *Mother Ruth's Rhymes* by Ruth I. Dowell.)

More Curriculum Connectors

 Because listening is related to the sense of hearing, these activities are also related to **science**.

 Sequencing is also a part of **mathematics**.

 Musical fingerplays like "Where Is Thumbkin?" and "The Eensy Weensy Spider" will connect the extended activity to **music**.

What Else I Did

_____

_____

_____

_____

_____

How Many Sounds?

What It Teaches

★   Auditory discrimination

★   Listening skills

★   Problem solving

What You'll Need

A sheet of 8½" x 11" paper

What to Do

★   Tell the children you're going to pass around a sheet of paper and you want each of them to create a different sound with it. (Possibilities include crumpling, tearing, flicking it with a finger, folding and unfolding, etc.)

How to Ensure Success

If the children get stumped, challenge them to use body parts other than the hands to create sounds. (Possibilities include rubbing the paper on the head, crumpling it underfoot, tapping it with a toe, blowing across it, or bouncing it off a knee.)

What Else You Can Do

★   Go on a "listening walk," asking the children to identify all the sounds they hear (for example, footsteps, automobiles, birds). When you get back to class, challenge them to depict the actions of some of the creatures and objects they heard.

★   You can also bring a tape recorder with you on a listening walk. When you return to the classroom, ask the children to first identify and then depict the sources of the sounds on the tape.

More Curriculum Connectors

 Listening is related to the sense of hearing, which is related to **science**.

 The creation of sounds is what **music** is all about.

What Else I Did

_____

_____

_____

_____

_____

What's That Sound?

What It Teaches

★ Auditory discrimination

★ Listening skills

What You'll Need

A variety of objects with familiar sounds (like rattling keys or chalk on a chalkboard); a tape recording of familiar sounds (optional)

What to Do

★ Ask the children to close their eyes, then make a sound with one of the objects.

★ Ask the children to identify the sound.

★ Challenge them to show you, through movement, the item creating the sound.

How to Ensure Success

Encourage the children to respond by either taking on the shape of the object identified or by performing its movement.

What Else You Can Do

★ An alternative is to make a tape recording of familiar sounds (for example, an electric can opener, a clock ticking, a door closing, or a vacuum cleaner) and play the tape for the children. This allows a broader range of sounds to be included in the activity.

★ Melody House offers an album called *El Mundo del Sonido (The World of Sound),* consisting of almost 70 different sounds. A 3-second space between sounds allows you to pause the recording so children can guess what they heard. The origin of the sound is then given, first in Spanish and then in English.

More Curriculum Connectors

 Listening is related to the sense of hearing, which also makes it part of **science**.

 The bilingual aspect of the second extension activity qualifies as **social studies**.

 Focused listening and auditory discrimination are also essential to **music**.

What Else I Did

_____

_____

_____

_____

_____

Speaking

Art ★ Language Arts ★ Mathematics ★ Music ★ Science ★ Social Studies

What's in a Name?

What It Teaches

★ The rhythm of words

★ An introduction to syllables

What You'll Need

No equipment needed

What to Do

★ Sit in a circle with the children and explain that they're going to discover the rhythm of their names.

★ Go around the circle, clapping one child's name at a time — one clap per syllable — as you say the name aloud. *Bobby Brown*, for example, would be Bob-by Brown: three claps with a pause between the second and third.

★ After you've spoken and clapped the rhythm of a name, the children, as a group, should echo.

How to Ensure Success

Say and clap the names as slowly as necessary.

Depending on the ages and developmental levels of your children, you may want to do both first and last names or first names only.

If the children have trouble echoing you, repeat the name until the majority are able to respond successfully.

Be sure the children are also saying the names aloud as they clap them.

What Else You Can Do

★ Once the children are able to clap the syllables of their names, add foot stamping — one stamp per syllable. Start with the children still seated, eventually graduating to stepping in place and, finally, to one step per syllable, moving around the room.

★   Once the children have mastered names, you can clap out the syllables of lines from nursery rhymes, poems, or favorite stories. For example, Ma-ry had a lit-tle lamb. Begin slowly, eventually increasing the tempo.

More Curriculum Connectors

 Rhythm is also a part of **music**.

 Point out the number of syllables in each child's name, perhaps even grouping the children by syllables (or letting them group themselves), to include **mathematics**.

What Else I Did

_____

_____

_____

_____

_____

Tell Me About . . .

What It Teaches

★ Connects cognitive, affective, and physical domains

★ Self-expression

★ Lends relevance to events in children's lives

What You'll Need

No equipment needed

What to Do

★ Choose a category you'd like to discuss with the children. For instance, you might ask them to tell you about their favorite birthday present, what they enjoyed most about their weekend, their favorite animal, etc.

★ Ask one child to verbally relate her or his response to your question. Then ask her or him to demonstrate through movement.

★ Ask the rest of the children to imitate the movement.

★ Repeat, giving each child a turn to initiate the discussion and movement.

How to Ensure Success

Encourage the children to either take on the shape of, for example, a favorite animal or perform its movements. Similarly, they could show you the shape of a favorite gift or depict its function. This allows the children to demonstrate either animate or inanimate favorites.

Because this is a rather lengthy process, you might choose to do this activity over several days rather than in one sitting in order to prevent restlessness.

What Else You Can Do

★ Acting out fairy tales and nursery rhymes increases the children's comprehension and helps them recall the order of events. And it's fun. Nursery rhymes like "Jack and Jill," "Humpty Dumpty," and "Jack Be Nimble" (which also provides practice with jumping) are great for dramatization. Children's books lending themselves to dramatization include *Caps for Sale, The Napping House,* and *Stellaluna,* to name a few. Ask the children to tell you about their favorite parts or their favorite characters and then depict their responses in movement.

More Curriculum Connectors

 Taking on shapes is related to **art**.

  Talking about holidays, families, and such is part of **social studies,** while discussing animals is relevant to **science**.

What Else I Did

_____

_____

_____

_____

_____

Four Voices

What It Teaches

★ Introduction to the "four voices"

★ Self-expression

What You'll Need

No equipment needed

What to Do

★ Explain to the children that there are four different ways of using the human voice: whispering, speaking, shouting, and singing.

★ Ask them to tell you which is loudest and which is softest. If they were to think of whispering and shouting in terms of size, which would be biggest? What do they think the difference between speaking and singing is? If they were to think of speaking and singing in terms of lines, which would be straight and which would be curvy?

★ Tell the children to each say their names (you can do this one child at a time or have everyone do it at once) in each of the four voices.

★ Assign a particular kind of movement — perhaps with the children's collaboration — to each of the four voices. For example, whispering might be tiptoeing, speaking could be represented by a simple walk, shouting by a forceful jump, and singing by a light run in a curving pathway.

★ Call out the kinds of voices, one at a time, challenging each child to say his or her name while performing the corresponding movement.

How to Ensure Success

This activity might be too much for your group to handle all at once. If so, you can concentrate on one type of voice per day.

Demonstrate the four voices with your own name if you feel it would be helpful to the children. You could also ask them to echo what you do so they understand.

Be as direct in your instruction as you need to be, based on the children's developmental levels. In other words, if they need you to remind them of the movement corresponding to the voice, then that's what you should do.

What Else You Can Do

★ Ask the children, one at a time, to demonstrate a movement representing one of the four voices — without any accompanying sound. Ask the rest of the children to guess the voice.

More Curriculum Connectors

 The concept of four voices is also part of **music**.

  Biggest and smallest are **mathematical** concepts, while straight and curvy lines are relevant to **art**.

Self-expression falls under the heading of **social studies**.

What Else I Did

_____

_____

_____

_____

_____

UNIT 8
Reading

Art ★ Language Arts ★ Mathematics ★ Music ★ Science ★ Social Studies

Action!

What It Teaches

★   Word comprehension

★   Self-expression

What You'll Need

A list of action words (possibilities include traveling words such as pounce, stamp, waddle, sneak, bounce, float, and slither; nontraveling action words include melt, collapse, shrink, shake, wriggle, and spin); a story with one or more action words in it (optional)

What to Do

★   Post your list of action words, discussing what the children think each of them means.

★   As you call out a word, the children perform the corresponding action.

How to Ensure Success

Of course, you'll want to start with words the children know well or can readily understand. When necessary, demonstrate.

At first, alternate only a few words at a time. Add more as the children are ready.

Include some stopping action words as well. Possibilities include freeze, pause, stop, and flop.

What Else You Can Do

★   Choose a story with one or more action words. After reading it aloud, choose a section including the word(s), asking the children to act it out. Children's stories like *The Little Engine That Could* and *Rosie's Walk* are among those that lend themselves to movement.

★   When the children are ready, increase the challenge by presenting two words at a time. The children then create their own combinations, performing as many repetitions of each as desired, in any order.

More Curriculum Connectors

 Self-expression falls under the heading of **social studies**.

What Else I Did

_____

_____

_____

_____

_____

Descriptive Words

What It Teaches

★   Word comprehension

★   Self-expression

What You'll Need

A list of descriptive words (possibilities include words such as graceful, light, forceful, smooth, droopy, gentle, strong, floppy, careful, enormous, tiny, and excited)

What to Do

★   Post your list, discussing what the children think each of the words means.

★   As you call out a word, the children perform a corresponding action.

How to Ensure Success

Start with words the children know well or can readily understand. Ask the children to tell you about times they might have felt some of these things. If necessary, demonstrate.

At first, alternate only a few words at a time. Add more as the children are ready.

What Else You Can Do

★   Ask the children to depict a person, character, animal, or object matching one of your descriptive words. For example, a giant is generally enormous, while a sad person might be droopy.

★   Children love to make up nonsense words. Ask each child to make one up and, after saying it, to demonstrate what it means.

More Curriculum Connectors

 Self-expression is an important early part of **social studies**.

 To include **art**, ask the children to draw something fitting one of the descriptive words.

What Else I Did

_____

_____

_____

_____

_____

Happy Endings

What It Teaches

★   Word comprehension

★   An introduction to suffixes

★   Self-expression

What You'll Need

No equipment needed

What to Do

★   Talk to the children about the difference between words like *frightened* and *frightening, scared* and *scary, squeezed* and *squeezing, collapsed* and *collapsing*.

★   Present the children with one word at a time, challenging them to demonstrate the appropriate action or posture. Follow that with the same word with a different suffix. Are the children able to show you the difference in meaning?

How to Ensure Success

At this point, the children don't need to hear the word *suffixes*. You can use the word *endings* instead to avoid confusing them.

As you present each word, provide as much description or imagery as necessary to enhance comprehension. For example, you might be *scared* if you were watching a monster movie, but you'd be *scary* if you were the monster!

What Else You Can Do

★   Make up a brief story that includes one word with different suffixes, directing the children to act it out as you tell it.

More Curriculum Connectors

 Self-expression is related to **social studies**.

What Else I Did

_____

_____

_____

_____

_____

Art ★ Language Arts ★ Mathematics ★ Music ★ Science ★ Social Studies

Left to Right

What It Teaches

★ Preparation for writing (and reading)

★ Spatial awareness

★ Laterality

★ Crossing the midline

What You'll Need

No equipment needed

What to Do

★ Have all the children sit or stand, facing the same direction.

★ Use objects or places in the room to indicate which is their left side and which is their right side. For example, they may be sitting with the windows to their left and the door to their right.

★ Challenge them to perform the following activities — and others like them — always moving from left to right (for example, from the windows toward the door):

    ★ Turning the head

    ★ Drawing a line on the floor with a foot

    ★ Moving both arms at various levels in space (e.g., at shoulder height, above the head, etc.)

    ★ Stepping (have them take several steps in a row)

    ★ Jumping, hopping, or sliding (depending on skill levels)

How to Ensure Success

Before each activity, remind the children that they're to execute the movement from, for example, the side the windows are on to the side the door is on. Using the words *left to right* in conjunction with these physical reminders will help make the concept less abstract for them.

If necessary, you can demonstrate the movements until the children are able to be successful on their own. If you do, be sure to sit or stand with your back to them so you're facing the same direction or, if you face them, remember to move from your right to left.

What Else You Can Do

★   When they're ready, challenge the children to perform group activities that involve left to right movement(s). For example, they can hold hands and circle to the right, hold hands in a line and slide left to right, or perform the "wave" from left to right.

More Curriculum Connectors

 The spatial awareness involved is also part of **art**.

 Any group activity involves cooperation, which is a component of **social studies**.

What Else I Did

_____

_____

_____

_____

_____

Show Me the Letter . . .

What It Teaches

★ Letter recognition

★ Ability to physically replicate what the eyes see

What You'll Need

The letters of the alphabet, for display; large, cut-out, lowercase letters (optional)

What to Do

★ Talk with the children about the straight, curving, and angled lines comprising the various letters of the alphabet.

★ Choose a letter, point it out to the children, and ask them to make the letter with their bodies. Repeat with several letters.

How to Ensure Success

Some letters are easier to replicate than others; begin with these. The fewer lines the letter has, the easier it is to reproduce. Some of the easiest are I, T, C, L, O, V, and X.

Allow the children to create either upper- or lowercase letters.

What Else You Can Do

★ When the children are ready to cooperate with others, have them form letters in pairs and, finally, trios. (Letters with three lines, like H, are fun to do in trios.)

★ For those children who are developmentally ready, you can ask them to work in small groups to create short words, such as *hi* or *cat*.

★ Scatter large letters on the floor throughout the room. Tell the children you're going to give them a locomotor skill to perform. On your signal, they move to any letter on the floor by executing the designated motor skill. Once at the letter, they take on its shape. Assign a new locomotor skill. At your next signal, the children move to new letters. The game continues until the children have moved, in as many different ways, to as many letters as possible. (Eventually, you can add adjectives to the game. For example, you might instruct the children to jog *slowly* to the next letter.)

More Curriculum Connectors

 Exploring shape is also part of **art**.

 Straight, curving, and angled lines are also explored in basic geometry, which falls under the heading of **mathematics**.

 Cooperating with others comes under the heading of **social studies**.

 To include **music**, choose "Marching Around the Alphabet" from Hap Palmer's *Learning Basic Skills Through Music,* Volume I, or *ABCs in Bubbaville,* available from Kimbo.

What Else I Did

_____

_____

_____

_____

_____

Skywriting

What It Teaches

★   Preparation for writing

★   Spatial awareness

What You'll Need

The alphabet, posted where the children can easily see it; recordings of various styles of music (optional)

What to Do

★   Ask the children to imagine the air in front of them is a giant chalkboard and they've got a big piece of chalk — in any color they like — in their hands.

★   Ask them to choose a letter from the alphabet and to "write" it on the "chalkboard."

★   Continue with other letters. Can they write short words or perhaps their names?

How to Ensure Success

Encourage the children to make their letters as large as possible at first, gradually writing them smaller and smaller.

Allow the children to make either upper- or lowercase letters.

What Else You Can Do

★   Ask the children to imagine the floor in front of them is the chalkboard and they have chalk at the end of their toes. Can they make the letters with a foot?

★   Once the children can do this, encourage them to use other body parts to "write." (Possibilities include elbows, the top of the head, the nose, and knees.)

★   Have one child at a time write a letter. Ask the rest of the class to guess the letter.

More Curriculum Connectors

 The spatial awareness involved in these activities also falls under the heading of **art**.

 Playing various styles of **music** in the background during these activities will not only add another content area to the mix, but it will also change the way the children create their letters. For example, many classical or New Age pieces inspire long, smooth strokes, while rock and roll tends to inspire short, jabbing lines.

What Else I Did

_____

_____

_____

_____

_____

MATHEMATICS

Art ★ Language Arts ★ Mathematics ★ Music ★ Science ★ Social Studies

To many adults, math is the most abstract of the content areas. We may have an aversion to this content area because we have failed in the past to do well in subjects like algebra and calculus or on standardized tests (I.Q. or SATs), which concentrate heavily on areas related to the logical/mathematical intelligence (Gardner, 1983; Armstrong, 1993). We may consider balancing a checkbook or staying within a budget a complicated process.

But young children don't view math the same way we do; for them, it is not abstract. As Essa (1992, p.270) explains, "The foundations of math are grounded in concrete experience such as the exploration of objects and gradual understanding of their properties and relationships. The cognitive concepts . . . of classification, seriation (ordering), numbers, time, and space all contribute to the gradual acquisition of math concepts."

Thus, children are acquiring mathematical knowledge (Mayesky, 1995; Essa, 1992) when they sort, stack, and compare manipulatives; play with sand and water; measure or set the table in the housekeeping center; or learn nursery rhymes and stories such as "The Three Little Kittens" and "Goldilocks and the Three Bears."

Quantitative ideas are also part of the language of mathematics. Mayesky (1995) recommends the following words be incorporated into the children's daily routine:

big and little	few	bunch
long and short	tall and short	group
high and low	light and heavy	pair
wide and narrow	together	many
late and early	same length	more
first and last	highest	twice
middle	lowest	
once	longer than	

Obviously, physical activity can help children attach meaning to these words, as well as to numerals and other mathematical concepts, so mathematics can continue to be a concrete rather than an abstract subject.

The mathematical concepts appropriate for exploration with young children include quantitative ideas, number awareness and recognition, counting, basic geometry, and simple addition and subtraction.

Quantitative and Positional Concepts

Art ★ Language Arts ★ Mathematics ★ Music ★ Science ★ Social Studies

The Long and the Short of It

What It Teaches

★   Quantitative concepts

★   Comparison

★   Opposites

What You'll Need

Straws or strips of paper in varying lengths and widths (optional)

What to Do

★   Ask the children to demonstrate the following with their bodies: big, small, high, low, long, short, tall, wide, and narrow.

★   Have them pair up, with partners demonstrating each of the following opposites: big/small, high/low, long/short, tall/short, and wide/narrow.

★   Still working in pairs, ask them to demonstrate concepts such as: same length, longer than, shorter than, taller than, higher than, and wider than.

How to Ensure Success

It may be helpful to use visual aids for these activities. For example, you could use straws in varying lengths to display long, short, longer than, and shorter than. You could use strips of paper to demonstrate wide versus narrow.

You may want to spread these activities over several sessions.

What Else You Can Do

★   After the children have experienced success with the preceding activities, challenge them to discover opposites for themselves. In other words, ask the children to demonstrate a wide shape. Once they have done so, ask them to show you the opposite of wide — without telling them what that is.

★   With the children working in pairs, one partner chooses a shape to demonstrate and the other depicts its opposite.

More Curriculum Connectors

 These concepts also fall under the content area of **art**.

 Opposites are a component of **language arts**. You can also incorporate Tana Hoban's book, *Opposites,* into your lesson.

 Comparisons are often necessary in understanding certain **science** concepts.

 Working in partners constitutes **social studies**.

What Else I Did

_____

_____

_____

_____

_____

Light and Heavy

What It Teaches

★ Quantitative concepts

★ Contrasting extremes

★ The movement element of force

What You'll Need

Lightweight scarf or feather (optional)

What to Do

★ Ask the children to sit and tap their fingers lightly on the floor in front of them. Then, in contrast, have them pound their fists on the floor. Continue to alternate between the two.

★ Challenge the children to move their arms as lightly as possible, as though their arms were butterfly wings. Ask them to pretend their arms are the propellers on a helicopter. Repeat several times.

★ Have the children stand and show you what they'd look like if they were statues made of metal. What would they look like if they were rag dolls? Can they feel the difference in their muscles? Alternate calling out "statues" and "rag dolls," varying the amount of time in between.

★ Ask the children to move as lightly as they can around the room, perhaps imagining they're walking on eggs and don't want to break them. Then ask them to move while making as much noise with their feet as they possibly can.

How to Ensure Success

Use whatever imagery you feel will help the children relate best to the concepts of light and heavy. For example, you may want to contrast a stalking cat with a dinosaur or a huge elephant for the last activity.

While most children will have no problem with heavy — or strong — movements, they may find moving lightly requires more control. To help inspire light movement, use a lightweight scarf or a feather to demonstrate.

What Else You Can Do

★ Use action words that inspire light or heavy movements. For light, the possibilities include *tiptoe, stalk, float, flutter,* and *glide*. For heavy, the possibilities include *stomp, stamp, pounce, crash,* and *pound*. Talk about the meanings of these words before asking the children to demonstrate them.

★ Use recorded music that corresponds to some of the preceding words or use a drum or tambourine to signal changes from one kind of action to another. For example, slowly bang on the drum to inspire stomping and tap more quickly on it to inspire tiptoeing.

More Curriculum Connectors

 Exploring the extremes in the muscle tension required of light and strong movements qualifies as **science**.

 Action words fall under the heading of **language arts**.

 The final extension activity brings **music** into the mix.

What Else I Did

_____

_____

_____

_____

_____

One More Time

What It Teaches

★ Quantitative concepts

★ Basic counting

★ Problem solving

★ Practice with nonlocomotor skills

What You'll Need

One piece of paper and pencil per child (optional)

What to Do

★ Choose any nonlocomotor skill (e.g., bending, shaking, swaying, or swinging) you wish the children to practice. Ask them to execute the skill once. Challenge them to do it one more time. How many times have they performed the skill? Challenge them to do it twice more. Do they know how many they've performed now?

★ Challenge them to find how many ways they can bend (or sit or turn), counting as they explore. How many body parts can they shake (or stretch or swing)?

How to Ensure Success

If the children have difficulty keeping track of their "discoveries," provide them each with a piece of paper and a pencil, directing them to make a slash mark for every possibility. Then help them tally their results.

What Else You Can Do

★ Challenge the children to discover which body part has the most possibilities for shaking (or bending or stretching or swinging). This requires a higher level of problem solving.

More Curriculum Connectors

 Comprehension of these quantitative terms also constitutes **language arts.**

 Exploration and discovery of this sort falls under the scope of **science**.

What Else I Did

_____

_____

_____

_____

_____

Me and My Shadow

What It Teaches

★ Positional concepts

★ General space

★ Practice with locomotion

★ Cooperation

What You'll Need

Carpet squares (optional)

What to Do

★ Have the children take partners. One child stands in front of the other, with both children facing the same direction. The child in front is going to lead her or his partner throughout the room, with the partner in back "shadowing" every move. After a while, the children reverse leads. (Be sure to use the words *in front of* and *behind* in your descriptions.)

How to Ensure Success

Talk to the children about shadows before undertaking this activity.

In order to ensure variety of movements, challenge the leaders to try different loco-motor skills, levels, pathways, and body shapes.

What Else You Can Do

★ Once the children have had ample practice in pairs, have them try this activity in groups of three (i.e., one leader and two shadows). Be sure to use the words *in the middle* and *between* in your descriptions. After a while, the first in line becomes the last in line, and so forth.

★ Give each child a carpet square to place on the floor, making sure they each have enough personal space. Issue challenges for the children to stand in various ways in relation to the carpet square. Possibilities include *on it*, *behind* it, *in front of* it, *beside* it, and *over* it.

More Curriculum Connectors

 The concept of shadows falls under the heading of **science**.

 Because the shadow game is a cooperative activity, it is also part of **social studies**.

 Exploring a variety of pathways, levels, and shapes constitutes **art**.

 The prepositions explored in these activities are a part of **language arts**.

What Else I Did

_____

_____

_____

_____

_____

Over the River and Through the Woods

What It Teaches

★ Positional concepts

★ Spatial awareness

★ Problem solving

What You'll Need

Materials for an obstacle course (e.g., classroom furniture, cardboard boxes, jump ropes, hoops); display cards with written or drawn directions

What to Do

★ Set up a simple obstacle course.

★ At each point on the course, display a card with a written or drawn direction (or both) indicating whether the children should move *over, under, around,* or *through* the obstacle.

★ Once the children have traversed the course several times, change it slightly. For example, rearrange the order of the obstacles. Also, if the children were previously expected to go *over* a hoop lying flat, you might stand the hoop in a holder and redirect them to travel *through* the hoop.

How to Ensure Success

Move through the course once yourself — with or without the children — to ensure they fully understand what's expected of them.

If you have a number of children waiting their turn, to avoid the disruptions that often result from impatience, give the children in line an assignment. For instance, have them create shapes with their bodies and body parts that someone or something could possibly move *over, under, around,* or *through.* If there's enough room, divide the class in half and have the two groups move through the course simultaneously, beginning on opposite sides.

What Else You Can Do

★ When the children are ready for more challenging problem solving, choose an item — like a hula hoop or a balance beam — and ask them to find two or three different ways to move *over, along,* or *beside* it.

★   You can further extend the activity by inviting the children to move, for instance, one-half, three-quarters, or two-thirds of the way across a balance beam. (Marking the beam with labeled pieces of masking tape ensures success.)

More Curriculum Connectors

 Because these positional concepts are prepositions, this activity also entails **language arts**.

 Spatial relationships are also involved, which relate to **art**.

 To reinforce these positional concepts, sing and discuss songs like "Over the River and Through the Woods," "Somewhere Over the Rainbow," "Ring Around the Rosie," "The Bear Went Over the Mountain," or "She'll Be Comin' 'Round the Mountain" **(music)**.

What Else I Did

_____

_____

_____

_____

_____

Number Awareness and Recognition

Number Shapes I

What It Teaches

★   Number awareness and recognition

★   Ability to physically replicate what the eyes see

★   Experience with the movement element of shape

What You'll Need

The numbers 0 through 9, for posting; large cut-out numbers (optional)

What to Do

★   Talk with the children about the straight, curving, and angled lines comprising the different numbers.

★   Choose a number, point it out to the children, and ask them to make the number with their bodies. Repeat with several numbers.

How to Ensure Success

Some numbers are easier to replicate than others; begin with these. The fewer lines the number has, the easier it is to reproduce. Some of the easiest are 0, 1, and 7.

Allow the children to create the numbers with the body as a whole or with body parts.

What Else You Can Do

★   Once the children are familiar with this concept, encourage them to try creating the numbers at different levels, such as standing, kneeling, sitting, and lying.

★   Ask the children to demonstrate the number that represents their age or to choose a number between, for example, 0 and 4 or 5 and 9.

★   When the children are ready to cooperate with others, have them form numbers in pairs and, finally, trios. (Numbers with three lines, like 4, are fun to do in trios.)

★ Place large numbers on the floor throughout the room. At your signal, the children move in a predesignated way (e.g., galloping) to any number they want, taking on the shape of that number once they arrive. Change the way in which they're to move to another number, give the signal again, and the game continues.

More Curriculum Connectors

 Exploring shape is also part of **art**.

 Cooperating with others comes under the heading of **social studies**.

 Volume I of Hap Palmer's *Learning Basic Skills Through Music* includes "The Number March," and Melody House offers an album called *Number Fun* **(music)**.

What Else I Did

_____

_____

_____

_____

_____

Number Shapes II

What It Teaches

★ Number awareness and recognition

★ Ability to physically replicate what the eyes see

★ Shapes

★ Practice with locomotor skills

What You'll Need

The numbers 0 through 9, for posting; one jump rope per child

What to Do

★ Provide each child with a jump rope, or something similar, with which to create the number you designate on the floor.

★ Once the number is ready, challenge the children to trace its pathway with a locomotor skill that you select.

How to Ensure Success

Begin with those numbers with the simplest shapes.

Choose only the locomotor skills the children can most easily perform.

If the children aren't developmentally ready to form the numbers themselves, create them yourself, perhaps even using a less temporary material, like masking tape.

What Else You Can Do

★ Allow the children to choose their own numbers and even their own locomotor skills.

★ A more advanced activity, if your children are doing simple computation, is to challenge them to create the number they get when adding, for instance, 1 plus 1.

More Curriculum Connectors

 Art is again incorporated through the exploration of shape.

 Physically replicating — that is, "writing" the numbers on the floor — links this activity to **language arts**.

What Else I Did

_____

_____

_____

_____

_____

Invisible Numbers

What It Teaches

★   Number awareness and recognition

★   Preparation for writing

★   Spatial awareness

What You'll Need

No equipment needed

What to Do

★   Ask the children to imagine the air in front of them is a giant chalkboard and they've got a big piece of chalk — in any color they like — in their hands.

★   Ask them to choose a number and "write" it on the "chalkboard."

★   Continue with other numbers, asking the children to vary the numbers' sizes.

How to Ensure Success

Encourage the children to make their numbers as large as possible at first, gradually writing them smaller and smaller.

Begin with the simplest numbers (those with the fewest lines, like 0 and 1) before moving on to numbers more difficult to draw (like 5).

What Else You Can Do

★   Ask the children to imagine the floor in front of them is the chalkboard and they have chalk at the end of their toes. Can they make the numbers with a foot?

★   Once the children can accomplish this, encourage them to use other body parts to "write" — on the chalkboard in the air or on the floor. Possible body parts include elbows, the top of the head, the nose, and the knees.

★   Have one child at a time write a number. Ask the rest of the class to guess the number.

More Curriculum Connectors

 The spatial awareness involved in these activities also falls under the heading of **art**.

 Preparation for writing constitutes **language arts**.

 If you play various styles of **music** in the background during these activities, you'll not only add another content area to the mix, but will also change the style with which the children create their letters. However, to make a true cognitive connection, talk with the children about the different qualities of the music and how those qualities made them feel like writing.

What Else I Did

_____

_____

_____

_____

_____

Counting

Art ★ Language Arts ★ Mathematics ★ Music ★ Science ★ Social Studies

Blast Off!

What It Teaches

- ★ Counting backward
- ★ Number awareness
- ★ Spatial awareness

What You'll Need

No equipment needed

What to Do

- ★ Ask the children to squat low, pretending to be spaceships on their launching pads.
- ★ With as much drama as you can muster, count backward from 10 to 1.
- ★ When you say "Blast off," the children "launch" themselves upward and pretend to fly around in outer space.
- ★ Repeat several times.

How to Ensure Success

Talk to the children about space shuttles, launching pads, and blasting off prior to the activity.

Let the children know when to expect to hear "Blast off."

Emphasize that, once the "spaceships" are in the air, they must maintain their own "personal space" in order not to collide.

What Else You Can Do

- ★ Call out every other number yourself, with the children supplying the missing ones. Eventually, have them do all the counting themselves.
- ★ Use the "blast off" part of this exercise every time you're moving from an activity that takes place sitting to one in which you want the children to stand.

More Curriculum Connectors

 The concept of space travel is part of **science**.

 The spatial awareness involved, particularly the levels through which the children move, is a component of **art**.

 Any discussion of astronaut as a choice of occupation would fall under the heading of **social studies**.

 Add a **language arts** component by reading Molly Bang's *Ten, Nine, Eight*.

What Else I Did

_____

_____

_____

_____

_____

How Many Parts?

What It Teaches

- ★ Counting
- ★ Body awareness
- ★ Divergent problem solving
- ★ Balance

What You'll Need

No equipment needed

What to Do

- ★ Challenge the children to place a certain number of body parts on the floor.
- ★ Repeat several times, varying the number of body parts. Also, sometimes challenge them to use the same number but different parts. For example, a challenge to touch the floor with three body parts could result in two feet and a hand, two hands and a foot, two knees and a hand, etc.

How to Ensure Success

Begin with higher numbers (but not too high; perhaps 5 being the highest) so the children won't have trouble with balance.

Be sure to point out the variety of responses you see so the children understand there are many "correct" possibilities.

Because children think differently than we do, they may not always count body parts as we would. For example, sometimes the bottom is counted as one part and sometimes as two. Sometimes, for young children, a foot counts as five parts. Be sure you understand *what* and *how* they're counting before you determine they have a problem with it.

Sometimes, rather than labeling the parts you see (e.g., "I see Leanne is using two elbows and two knees"), count body parts as you move throughout the room. Of course, if you've asked them to place four parts on the floor, you should be counting 1 to 4 repeatedly; the repetition is helpful to the children.

What Else You Can Do

★   Ask the children to count the number of seconds they can hold very still in
each position. Once they're more adept at balance, challenge them to see how
many seconds they can balance in each position.

More Curriculum Connectors

 Identifying body parts and balance are **science** concepts, as is finding
the center of gravity, which the children must do if they're going to
remain upright.

 Language arts possibilities include Laurent de Brunhoff's *Babar's
Counting Book, The Doorbell Rang* by Pat Hutchins, *Count!* by Denise
Fleming, and *A Caribbean Counting Book* by Faustin Charles and
Roberta Arenson, which adds a cultural component, linking it to **social
studies**.

What Else I Did

_____

_____

_____

_____

_____

Oh, the Possibilities

What It Teaches

★ Counting

★ Problem solving

★ Body awareness

What You'll Need

No equipment needed

What to Do

★ Ask the children to discover how many ways they can move an arm, for example.

★ Give them ample time to explore and then repeat with a different body part. Possible parts include a leg, the head, a hand, or a shoulder.

How to Ensure Success

If the children need some extra help from you, suggest they try moving the parts in different directions and at different levels.

If necessary, you can explore, discover, and count with them.

The arm and hand would probably be the easiest parts with which to begin. Moving just one leg requires balance, and the head and shoulder require a certain amount of body part isolation, which is challenging for young children.

What Else You Can Do

★ Ask the children to discover how many steps (jumps, hops, etc.) it takes to get from one end of the room (or movement space) to the other.

★ Does the number change if they cross diagonally?

More Curriculum Connectors

 Exploration and discovery, as well as problem solving, are vital to the nature of **science**.

 The spatial awareness involved in the alternate activity is a component of **art**.

What Else I Did

_____

_____

_____

_____

_____

Basic Geometry

Art ★ Language Arts ★ Mathematics ★ Music ★ Science ★ Social Studies

Line 'Em Up

What It Teaches

★ Basic geometry involving lines

★ Shape

★ Body awareness

★ Ability to physically replicate what the eyes see

What You'll Need

Drawings of vertical, horizontal, diagonal, crossed, curved, and crooked lines; masking tape, to create the various lines on the floor (optional)

What to Do

★ Post the drawings of lines where the children can see them.

★ Discuss each of these lines with your group.

★ Ask the children to replicate each with their bodies or with individual body parts.

How to Ensure Success

When discussing the various lines, use imagery and phrases the children can relate to. For instance, a vertical line might be said to be "standing up," while a horizontal line is "lying down." Use the corners of the room when describing a diagonal line, which goes from corner to corner.

Begin with the simplest lines, which are vertical and horizontal. The most challenging are going to be diagonal and crossed.

What Else You Can Do

★ Place masking tape on the floor, replicating the various types of lines, and ask the children to move along them. Begin with such basic locomotor skills as creeping or walking, changing the skill every time the children complete one pass. A more advanced challenge is to assign a different locomotor skill for each type of line.

★ Challenge the children to create the lines with partners.

★ Ask the children to discover examples of the different lines throughout the room. Then present such challenges as, "Show me the kind of line made by the flagpole."

More Curriculum Connectors

 Shape and line also fall under the heading of **art**.

 Working in cooperation with a partner constitutes **social studies**.

 The ability to physically replicate what the eyes see is necessary in writing, which is part of **language arts**.

What Else I Did

_____

_____

_____

_____

_____

On the Right Path

What It Teaches

- ★ Recognition of lines
- ★ Pathways
- ★ Practice with locomotor skills

What You'll Need

Masking tape, rope, chalk, or something similar to create pathways on the floor (optional); carpet squares or hoops (optional)

What to Do

- ★ Beginning with the locomotor skill of walking, ask the children to travel about the room. Challenge them to first move only in straight paths.
- ★ Once the children have succeeded in traveling in straight pathways, ask them to make curving and, finally, zigzagging pathways.
- ★ Follow the same pattern with other locomotor skills (run, jump, leap, gallop, hop, slide, and skip).

How to Ensure Success

Demonstrate straight, curving, and zigzag pathways for the children, perhaps initially playing a brief game of Follow the Leader.

If necessary, create the three types of pathways on the floor with masking tape, chalk, or rope.

What Else You Can Do

- ★ Challenge the children to move along straight, curving, and zigzag pathways in backward and sideward directions.
- ★ Play a game called Come to Me. In this game, the children scatter throughout the room, each finding her or his own personal space (if the children will have trouble remembering where their spots are, provide them with carpet squares

or hoops). You then stand in the center of the room, instructing the children to come to you in various ways. For example, to gain additional practice with pathways you might say, "Come to me, traveling in a straight path from your spot." Once all the children have arrived at your spot, give them instructions for returning to their personal spaces (e.g., "Return to your personal space, traveling in a curvy pathway"). Once the children are handling one instruction at a time, increase the challenge by combining two instructions (e.g., "Come to me at a low level, moving in a zigzagging pathway").

More Curriculum Connectors

 The concept of line also falls under the heading of **art**.

What Else I Did

_____

_____

_____

_____

_____

Right to the Point

What It Teaches

★ Recognition of points

★ Shape

★ Body awareness

What You'll Need

Miscellaneous items found throughout the classroom

What to Do

★ Show the children examples of different points found in the room (e.g., the point of a pencil, the corner of the chalkboard, the point of a clock hand, the corner of a book).

★ Ask the children to first create a pointed shape with their fingers. Advance from there by challenging them to create pointed shapes with their arms and hands, their feet, and their body as a whole.

How to Ensure Success

Speaking in terms of pointed *shapes,* instead of simply creating points, should make things clearer to the children.

If necessary, demonstrate several pointed shapes yourself.

What Else You Can Do

★ Ask the children to create pointed shapes in pairs and trios.

More Curriculum Connectors

 The concept of points is essential to **art**.

 Working in pairs and trios constitutes **social studies**.

What Else I Did

_____

_____

_____

_____

_____

What a Square!

What It Teaches

- ★ Simple geometric shapes
- ★ Body awareness

What You'll Need

Pictures of circles, triangles, and squares; masking tape or rope (optional)

What to Do

- ★ Post the pictures where the children can easily see them.
- ★ Talk to the children about the straight and curving lines that make up each of these geometric shapes.
- ★ Ask the children to replicate these three shapes with their bodies or individual body parts.

How to Ensure Success

Point out that a circle is one continuous, curving line; a triangle is made up of three straight lines; and a square consists of four straight lines.

If necessary, first explore the possibilities for angles created by the body and body parts.

Encourage the children to create their shapes at various levels in space, such as lying, kneeling, and standing.

What Else You Can Do

- ★ Have the children create their shapes in groups of two, three, and four.
- ★ Create these shapes on the floor with masking tape or rope and ask the children to travel along the shapes using a variety of locomotor skills.
- ★ Show the children a rectangle and challenge them to show you, with their bodies, the difference between a rectangle and a square.

★ Challenge them to discover circles, triangles, squares, and rectangles through-out the room. Ask them to show you, for example, the shape of the door or the top of the wastebasket.

More Curriculum Connectors

 Art is also covered with these activities.

 Working in pairs or groups constitutes **social studies**.

 To include **language arts**, choose from Tana Hoban's books *Circles, Triangles, and Squares; Round, Round, Round;* and *Shapes, Shapes, Shapes.* Other possibilities are Eric Carle's *My First Book of Shapes* and John Reiss' *Shapes.*

What Else I Did

_____

_____

_____

_____

_____

Simple Computation

Art ★ Language Arts ★ Mathematics ★ Music ★ Science ★ Social Studies

"Roll Over"

What It Teaches

★   Subtraction

★   Practice with log rolls

★   Cooperation

What You'll Need

Floor mat; Merle Peek's *Roll Over: A Counting Book* (both optional)

What to Do

★   If the children aren't familiar with the song "Roll Over," teach them the lyrics and discuss the song with them. The lyrics are as follows:

There were 10 in the bed,
And the little one said,
"Roll over, roll over."
So they all rolled over,
And one fell out.

There were 9 in the bed
And the little one said . . .

One in the bed,
And the little one said,
"Alone at last!" (spoken)

★   Choose ten children to lie on the floor (or a floor mat, if possible), pretending they're lying in a bed. Then, as you and the remaining children sing the song, the children on the floor act it out.

★   Prior to each verse, ask the group to tell you how many children are remaining in the bed.

How to Ensure Success

Before starting the song, have the children practice log rolls. Explain that they should keep their bodies as straight as logs and "hide" their ears with their arms as they roll over, beginning and ending on their backs.

Practice "group rolling" with the children who are going to be "in the bed." Explain they shouldn't roll until they hear the lyrics "So they all rolled over."

You might want to start with a smaller group than ten.

If members of your group will feel left out if not included in the rolling, divide your class into groups of the same number and begin the song with that number. In other words, if you have 15 children in class, divide them into three groups of five; then start the song with "There were five in the bed."

What Else You Can Do

★   Merle Peek has illustrated this song in the book *Roll Over: A Counting Book.* You could use the book instead of, or in addition to, singing the song.

★   Act out the song "The Three Little Monkeys." The lyrics are as follows:

Three little monkeys
Jumping on the bed,
One fell off and bumped his head,
Mother called the doctor and the doctor said,
"No more monkeys jumping on the bed."

Two little monkeys
Jumping on the bed,
One fell off and bumped his head,
Mother called the doctor and the doctor said,
"No more monkeys jumping on the bed."

One little monkey
Jumping on the bed,
One fell off and bumped his head,
Mother called the doctor and the doctor said,
"Get those monkeys back to bed."

More Curriculum Connectors

 The song puts this activity under the heading of **music**.

 The cooperation involved in rolling over together constitutes **social studies**.

 The song lyrics are a part of **language arts**, which you'll be further addressing if you use the book suggested.

What Else I Did

_____

_____

_____

_____

_____

Add 'Em and Subtract 'Em

What It Teaches

★ Counting

★ Simple addition and subtraction

★ Levels in space

What You'll Need

Numbered cards (optional)

What to Do

★ Have the children sit in a circle on the floor.

★ Call out a child's name. The child then gets up and stands in the center of the circle.

★ Ask the children how many are in the center. When they've responded correctly, call out another child's name. That child joins the child already in the center.

★ Ask the children how many are in the circle now.

★ Continue adding — and subtracting — children, each time asking the group to tell you how many are standing in the center.

How to Ensure Success

Begin by adding and subtracting only one child at a time. Later, when the children are ready, add or subtract two or three children at a time.

Be sure to use the words *add* and *subtract* in your game. For example, you might say, "We've added *one* person to the *one* already in the circle. How many are in the circle now?"

You might want to call out the children's names in the order in which they're sitting (perhaps nearest to farthest from you) so they don't get the feeling you're choosing favorites first. Another way is to close your eyes and point.

What Else You Can Do

★ Vary the locomotor skills used to enter and leave the circle. You can assign a skill or let the children choose.

★ Instead of playing this game in a circle, call the children by name — one, two, or three at a time — to the front of the room. When it's time to subtract children, simply ask them to return to their seats. Call the game Stand Up, Sit Down.

★ If your children are ready for more challenging computation, give each of them a number written on a card. Call two children at a time to the center of the circle (or front of the room), and ask the remaining children to add (or subtract) the numbers on the cards.

More Curriculum Connectors

Whichever version of the game you play, the children will be moving from low to high levels and back again. These positional concepts address not only another aspect of mathematics but **art** as well.

To add **music** to math lessons, consider Hap Palmer's *Math Readiness: Addition and Subtraction* and Alan Stern's *Sing a Sum . . . or a Remainder,* for first and second grades, both available from Educational Activities.

What Else I Did

_____

_____

_____

_____

_____

How Many Parts Now?

What It Teaches

★   Counting

★   Basic addition and subtraction

★   Body awareness

★   Balance

★   Divergent problem solving

What You'll Need

Floor mats (optional)

What to Do

★   This is a variation of "How Many Parts?" (presented previously), in which you asked the children to place certain numbers of body parts on the floor. With this game, you'll start off the same way but then ask the children to add or subtract one (or two or three) part(s) to those already touching the floor. For instance, begin by asking the children to put three body parts on the floor. Once they've accomplished this, ask them to add or subtract one body part.

★   After each challenge to add or subtract a part or parts, ask the children to tell you how many parts they now have touching the floor.

How to Ensure Success

Start by asking the children to place just two or three parts on the floor and to add or subtract from those.

At first, add or subtract only one body part at a time. When they're ready, move on to two and, finally, three parts.

Point out the different responses you see (e.g., one child might have a hand and a foot touching the floor, while another has chosen a knee and a hand) so the children understand there are lots of "right" answers.

What Else You Can Do

★ For more of a challenge, add and subtract numbers of body parts touching *each other*.

★ For a cooperative activity, call for a certain number of children to connect at the elbows, for example. Then add and subtract children from there. (Try to divide the class evenly so there aren't children left out. For instance, if you have fifteen in a class, group them by either threes or fives.)

More Curriculum Connectors

 Body awareness and balance are concepts that fall under **science**.

 Working cooperatively is part of **social studies**.

What Else I Did

_____

_____

_____

_____

_____

MUSIC

It's impossible to think of music and movement as completely separate entities. Music educator Carl Orff based his approach on the belief that music, movement, and speech are interrelated. Jaques-Dalcroze (1931, p. 115) felt traditional methods of training musicians concentrated too heavily on the intellect, thereby neglecting the senses. To him, "The most potent element in music and the nearest related to life is rhythmic movement."

Not only did educators like Dalcroze and Orff consider music and movement inseparable, but children do, too. For young children, experiencing music is simply not limited to the auditory sense (Isenberg & Jalongo, 1993; Haines & Gerber, 1992; Bayless & Ramsey, 1991), as evidenced by even infants' "whole-body" response to music.

Unfortunately, too often a child's musical ability is judged by an ability to sing or play an instrument (Driver, 1936). Even if a child possesses such talent, if his exposure to music is limited to one of these two avenues, he is not experiencing music to the fullest. What of the child who shows no interest in or aptitude for singing or playing an instrument?

If all children are to fully experience music, they should explore it as a whole, being given opportunities to listen, sing, play, create, and *move*. When a child tiptoes to soft music, stamps her feet to loud music, moves in slow motion to Bach's "Air on the G String" then rapidly to Rimsky-Korsakov's "Flight of the Bumblebee," sways to a 3/4 meter and skips to a piece in 6/8, she is experiencing the music on many levels. Not only is she listening, but she is using her body, mind, and spirit to express and create. Because she is using a multimodal approach, what she learns will make a lasting impression.

Some musical concepts are too advanced for young children to grasp. Others are important only to those who go on to study music seriously. But there are many musical elements young children can and should experience, including tempo, volume, staccato and legato, pitch, mood, and rhythm.

Tempo is the speed at which the music is performed, which means this musical element is related to the movement element of time. The best way to introduce tempo is by contrasting the extremes — very slow and very fast. Once children can recognize and move to fast and slow music, begin introducing the more challenging concept of the continuum from very slow to very fast and the reverse. *Accelerando* is the term for music that begins slowly and gradually increases in tempo. *Ritardando* indicates a gradually decreasing tempo.

Volume refers specifically to the loudness or softness of sounds. According to Haines and Gerber (1992, p. 157), many people incorrectly associate big or high movements with loud music and small, low movements with soft music. However, because volume is better equated with movement's "relative strength or weakness, its firmness or gentleness," this musical element truly goes hand in hand with the movement element of force. When the music is soft, moving with a great deal of muscle tension would be an unlikely response. On the other hand, when the music is loud, it isn't likely to conjure up, for example, images of butterflies floating. Again, the best way to introduce volume is by contrasting extremes. Once the children can move well to loud and soft music, begin introducing the continuum from one to the other. *Crescendo* is the term for music that begins softly and gradually gets louder. *Decrescendo* refers to a gradually decreasing volume.

Staccato and legato relate to the movement element of flow and are part of the broader category of articulation. *Legato*, which corresponds to free flow (smooth, uninterrupted movement), indicates the music is to be played without any noticeable interruptions between the notes. In other words, the music flows smoothly. *Staccato*, on the other hand, is more punctuated and therefore corresponds with bound flow (interrupted or halting).

Pitch is the highness or lowness of a musical tone. With this concept, the use of high and low movements are most appropriate.

Feelings are often conveyed by music and, very often, young children are the first to pick up on the mood of a song and to respond to it. This ability seems to be due to the as yet undiminished sensitivity of the young child's ear and to her or his as yet undiminished willingness to show a physical response. Your role as a teacher is to make the children aware of how different music affects them. Talk to them about how certain songs make them feel, the musical elements involved, and why they think the songs evoke the responses they do.

Rhythm, according to McDonald and Simons (1989, p. 290), is the "organization of sounds, silences, and patterns into different groupings." Within the context of this book, rhythm will consist of the concepts of beat and meter.

The *beat* in music is the recurring rhythmic pulse that is heard (and felt) throughout a piece. *Meter* indicates a basic group of beats. When a meter is stated, the top number refers to the number of beats in a measure; the bottom number indicates the *kind* of note that equals one beat. For example, 2/4 means there are two *quarter*-notes per measure, with 6/8 indicating six *eighth*-notes to the measure. A quarter-note can be likened to a walking step; it takes approximately the same time to complete. An eighth-note is twice as fast as a quarter-note (more like a running step).

All of these musical elements can be explored through movement, offering the children a multisensory approach that gives the concepts greater meaning and makes for greater retention.

UNIT 15

Tempo

Moving Slow/Moving Fast

What It Teaches

★ Recognition and contrast of tempos

★ Experience with the movement element of time

★ Listening skills

What You'll Need

A hand drum and mallet or an alternative (a coffee can or an oatmeal container with a lid and a wooden spoon will do)

What to Do

★ Talk to the children about very slow and very fast. What are some times when they would move in either way?

★ Ask the children to stand and move in the ways the drum makes them feel like moving. Then alternate between very slow and very fast beats.

How to Ensure Success

If the children have any trouble with this, offer suggestions of how they could move. For example, the slow beats might inspire giant steps, while the quick beats inspire tiny ones.

Be sure your beats demonstrate a vast difference between very slow and very fast. Contrasting extremes is the best way to introduce concepts like slow and fast.

When you want the children to move slowly, *speak* slowly. When you want them to move quickly, pick up the pace of your speech.

What Else You Can Do

★ The drum will inspire a great deal of excitement. Letting each child have a turn with it, dictating the group's movement, provides a real sense of power for them. (Don't worry if the children don't get the beating quite right at first.)

More Curriculum Connectors

 Listening skills are a part of the **language arts**.

 Listening is also related to the sense of hearing, which falls under the heading of **science**.

What Else I Did

_____

_____

_____

_____

_____

Moving Slow/Moving Fast — Again

What It Teaches

★ Recognition and contrast of tempos

★ Experience with the movement element of time

★ Listening skills

What You'll Need

A recording consisting of both very slow and very fast tempos (possibilities include "Slow and Fast" from Hap Palmer's *The Feel of Music;* "The Slow Fast, Soft Loud Clap Song" from Kimbo's *Songs About Me;* and "Moving Slow/Moving Fast" and "Marching Slow/Marching Fast" from Rae Pica's Moving & Learning Series) or two different recordings — one slow and one fast; streamers or scarves (optional)

What to Do

★ Play the recording(s) you've selected, pointing out the difference between the slow and fast tempos. Can the children think of some ways each would make them feel like moving?

★ Play the recording(s) again, this time challenging the children to move in a variety of ways to each tempo. Possibilities for the slow tempo include gentle swaying, walking through mud (or deep snow or peanut butter), pretending to be a turtle or snail, and pretending to be in a film that's being played in slow motion. For the fast tempo, possibilities are running lightly (in place or around the room), skipping, pretending to be a bumblebee, and pretending to be a race car.

How to Ensure Success

When you first start exploring tempo with the children, you may want to act out the movements with them. This may inspire imitation but will give them a sense of security. Then, as the children gain experience, refrain from participating. Be sure to point out the different responses you see so they understand it's okay to respond in different ways.

Be sure the pieces you choose demonstrate a vast difference between slow and fast.

Be sure to use imagery to which the children can relate.

What Else You Can Do

★ Provide the children with streamers or chiffon scarves, challenging them to show you how slowly or quickly the prop can move to the music.

★ Have the children select partners. Ask one partner to lead and the other to follow ("shadow") as the slow and fast music is played.

More Curriculum Connectors

 Listening skills are a necessary part of **language arts**.

 Listening is also related to the sense of hearing, which falls under the heading of **science**.

 The partner activity promotes cooperation, a part of **social studies**.

What Else I Did

_____

_____

_____

_____

_____

Slow to Fast and Back Again

What It Teaches

★ Recognition of the continuum from slow to fast (*accelerando*) and vice versa (*ritardando*)

★ Experience with the movement element of time

★ Physical control

★ Listening skills

What You'll Need

Hand drum and mallet or a substitute; music that accelerates or retards, or both (optional)

What to Do

★ With the children sitting and listening, begin by drumming very slowly. Then, gradually increase your tempo until it's very fast.

★ Now play a game of Follow the Leader, with you at the head of the line. Accompanying yourself with the drum (one beat for every step you take), begin to move very slowly. Gradually accelerate your tempo until you're going as fast as you want the children to go. Then begin to gradually slow down until you're back to the original speed.

How to Ensure Success

For both parts of this activity, verbally describe what you're doing as you're doing it. For example, "I'm beating the drum *very slowly* now."

Be sure your beats move from one extreme to the other gradually and steadily.

Being able to gradually increase the body's tempo to match the drum's (or the music's) is developmentally quite challenging and will require lots of repetition.

What Else You Can Do

★ To make the Follow the Leader game more challenging, eventually begin to vary your movements by changing levels, directions, pathways, and if possible, body shape.

★ Once the children are familiar with this concept, they can take turns as leader.

★ Try the activity to music that accelerates, retards, or does both.

More Curriculum Connectors

 Follow the Leader is a cooperative activity, which qualifies it as **social studies**.

 Being able to physically replicate what the eyes are seeing, as the children must do during Follow the Leader, is necessary in both **art** and **language arts**.

 Listening falls under the categories of **language arts** and **science**.

What Else I Did

_____

_____

_____

_____

_____

UNIT 16

Volume

Art ★ Language Arts ★ Mathematics ★ Music ★ Science ★ Social Studies

Moving Softly/Moving Loudly

What It Teaches

★ Recognition and contrast of volumes

★ Experience with the movement element of force

★ Listening skills

What You'll Need

Hand drum and mallet or substitute

What to Do

★ Talk to the children about very soft and very loud. What are some times when they speak softly or loudly? When do they move softly or loudly?

★ Ask the children to stand and move in the ways the drum makes them feel like moving. Then, alternate between very soft (light) and very loud (strong) beats.

How to Ensure Success

If the children have any trouble with this, you can offer suggestions of how they could move. For example, the soft beats might inspire tiptoeing, while the loud beats inspire stomping.

Be sure your beats demonstrate a vast difference between very soft and very loud. Contrasting extremes is the best way to introduce these concepts.

If you find you're having trouble beating the drum quietly enough, you can simply rub the mallet over the drumhead.

When you want the children to move softly, *speak* softly. When you want them to move strongly, increase the volume of your speech.

What Else You Can Do

★ Let each child have a turn with the drum, dictating the group's movement.

★ A more challenging version of this game is to use just your voice to inspire soft and loud movements. How does a whisper make the children feel like moving? A shout?

More Curriculum Connectors

 Listening skills are a part of the **language arts**, as are the two different voices (whispering and shouting) suggested in the alternate activity.

Listening is also related to the sense of hearing, which falls under the heading of **science**.

What Else I Did

_____

_____

_____

_____

_____

Moving Softly/Moving Loudly — Again

What It Teaches

★ Recognition and contrast of volumes

★ Experience with the movement element of force

★ Listening skills

What You'll Need

One recording consisting of both very soft and very loud volumes or two different recordings — one soft and one loud (children's songs offering contrast between soft and loud include "Soft and Loud" from Hap Palmer's *The Feel of Music;* "Play Soft, Play Loud" from Jill Gallina's *Rockin' Rhythm Band*; and "Moving Softly/ Moving Loudly" from Rae Pica and Richard Gardzina's Moving & Learning Series); maracas or shakers (optional)

What to Do

★ Play the recording(s) you've selected, pointing out the difference between the soft and loud volumes. How do the children imagine each would make them feel like moving?

★ Play the recording(s) again, this time challenging them to move in a variety of ways to each volume. Possibilities for the soft volume include tiptoeing, moving as quietly as a cat, pretending to sneak up on someone, or "floating." For the loud volume, possibilities are stamping the feet, slapping the floor, rocking forcefully, and moving like a dinosaur.

How to Ensure Success

When you first start exploring volume with the children, you may want to act out the movements with them. This may result in imitation but will give them a sense of security. Then, as the children gain experience, refrain from participating. Be sure to point out the different responses you see so they understand it's okay to respond in different ways.

Be sure the pieces you choose demonstrate a vast difference between soft and loud.

Be sure to use imagery to which the children can relate.

What Else You Can Do

★   Provide the children with maracas or shakers, challenging them to show you how softly or loudly the prop can move to the music.

★   Have the children select partners. Ask one partner to lead and the other to follow ("shadow") as the soft and loud music is played.

More Curriculum Connectors

 Listening skills are a necessary part of **language arts**.

 Listening is also related to the sense of hearing, which falls under the heading of **science**.

 The partner activity promotes cooperation, a part of **social studies**.

What Else I Did

_____

_____

_____

_____

_____

Soft to Loud and Back Again

What It Teaches

★ Recognition of the continuum from soft to loud (*crescendo*) and vice versa (*decrescendo*)

★ Experience with the movement element of force

★ Physical control

★ Listening skills

What You'll Need

Hand drum and mallet or a substitute; music that increases or decreases in volume, or both (optional) (Ravel's *Bolero* is a classic example of crescendo. From Grieg's *Lyric Suite,* "Norwegian Rustic March," both increases and decreases, as does "Getting Louder/Getting Softer" from Rae Pica's Moving & Learning Series.)

What to Do

★ With the children sitting and listening, begin by drumming very softly. Then, gradually increase your volume until it's very loud.

★ Now play a game of Follow the Leader, with you at the head of the line. Accompanying yourself with the drum (one beat for every step you take), begin to move very softly. Gradually increase your volume until you're going as "loudly" as you want the children to go. Then, begin to gradually decrease your volume until you're back to the original volume.

How to Ensure Success

For both parts of this activity, verbally describe what you're doing as you're doing it. For example, "I'm beating the drum *very softly* now."

Be sure your beats move from one extreme to the other gradually and steadily.

Being able to physically match the drum's (or the music's) increasing and decreasing volume is quite challenging and will require lots of repetition to ensure success.

What Else You Can Do

★ To make the Follow the Leader game more challenging, eventually begin to vary your movements by changing levels, directions, pathways, and if possible, body shape.

★ Once the children are familiar with this concept, they can take turns as leader.

★ Try the activity to music that gradually increases or decreases in volume, or does both. Or play a single piece of music that you start at a very soft volume, and gradually turn up the volume knob until the song is as loud as you want it to be.

More Curriculum Connectors

 Follow the Leader is a cooperative activity, which qualifies it as **social studies**.

 Being able to physically replicate what the eyes are seeing, as the children must do during Follow the Leader, is necessary in both **art** and **language arts**.

 Listening falls under the categories of **language arts** and **science**.

What Else I Did

_____

_____

_____

_____

_____

UNIT 17

Staccato and Legato

Art ★ Language Arts ★ Mathematics ★ Music ★ Science ★ Social Studies

"Pop Goes the Weasel"

What It Teaches

★ Bound flow

★ Listening skills

What You'll Need

A recording of "Pop Goes the Weasel" (optional)

What to Do

★ Play — or hum or sing — "Pop Goes the Weasel," instructing the children to walk along with it — until they hear the "pop." At the sound of the pop, they jump into the air and then continue walking.

★ Once the children have become accustomed to this, make the activity more challenging by instructing them to jump *and* change direction when they hear the pop.

How to Ensure Success

Even if you're using a recording, sing along with it, strongly emphasizing the pop.

You can "broadcast" the forthcoming pop with your posture and facial expressions.

Perform the activity with the children at first — and again when you've asked them to add the change in direction.

What Else You Can Do

★ To truly interrupt the flow of movement, challenge the children to freeze in their spots when they hear the pop. They can't start moving again until the phrase, ending with the word *weasel,* has finished.

★ Sing (or hum) the song, speeding up and slowing down indiscriminately so the children can't predict exactly when the pop will come. They should also match the tempo and flow ("choppy" or uninterrupted) to the manner in which you're performing the song.

More Curriculum Connectors

 Listening skills are a necessary part of **language arts**.

What Else I Did

_____

_____

_____

_____

_____

Statues

What It Teaches

★   Bound flow

★   Listening skills

★   Ability to differentiate between sound and silence

★   Ability to stop on signal

What You'll Need

Two or three songs with different musical styles (e.g., a recent Top 40 hit, a Strauss waltz, and an African or Latin piece with a strong beat); scarves, streamers, hoops, or foam balls (optional)

What to Do

★   Explain to the children that you're going to put on a piece of music. While the music's playing, they should move in any way they want. When the music stops (press the pause button on the tape or CD player or lift the needle off the record), they must also stop — immediately — and freeze into statues until the music begins again.

★   To take the children by surprise and inspire a variety of responses, vary the time you allow the children to move before stopping the music. (Don't always stop it at the end of a musical phrase.)

How to Ensure Success

Instead of asking the children to move "in the way the music makes them feel," which can be intimidating to many children, make it clear this is a game.

Before actually beginning the game, ask the children to show you what statues look like. What are some statues they might know about (the Statue of Liberty) or may have seen? Once they've assumed statue shapes, point out the tenseness of their muscles, as well as how still they are.

To expose your children to a variety of musical styles and rhythms, use a song with a different feel (a march, a waltz, rock and roll) each time you play Statues. Simply be sure the style you choose really lends itself to movement.

What Else You Can Do

★ Props are wonderful for alleviating self-consciousness (the focus is on the prop and not the child) and for adding a whole new dimension to an activity. Give your children lightweight scarves, streamers, hoops, or foam balls and ask them to show you how the music makes them feel like moving the prop.

★ Once your children feel absolutely comfortable "improvising" to music of varying styles, make a game out of simply moving to the music (without stopping it). This will give them some experience with the element of free flow.

More Curriculum Connectors

 Listening is one of the four components of **language arts**.

 Awareness of muscle tension is part of **science** for young children.

 Shape is an element of **art**.

What Else I Did

_____

_____

_____

_____

_____

Bound and Free

What It Teaches

★ The movement element of flow

★ Listening skills

What You'll Need

Recordings of pieces that are examples of staccato and legato (optional)

What to Do

★ Sing "Twinkle, Twinkle, Little Star" or "Row, Row, Row Your Boat" with the children.

★ Tell them you're going to sing it in different ways and that you want them to move in the way you're singing it.

★ Sing the song once through in a punctuated manner, adding pauses between syllables, to experience staccato. Ask the children how the "choppiness" of the song makes them feel like moving.

★ Sing the song again, only this time as smoothly and as flowing as possible, to experience legato. Does this make the children feel like moving differently?

How to Ensure Success

Prior to conducting this activity, challenge the children to depict certain things that move in bound and free-flowing ways. For example, you could ask them to show you how robots and butterflies move, alternating between the two. Be sure they demonstrate the muscle tension and punctuated movement of the robot and the floating easiness of the butterfly.

Demonstrate with your posture and facial expressions what you're expecting with each version of the song. For example, with the staccato version, you should be tense. With the legato, you want to show relaxation in your muscles.

What Else You Can Do

★ Choose recordings that demonstrate both staccato and legato. For instance, portions of Haydn's *Surprise Symphony* are staccato, while "Aquarium" from Saint-Saens' *Carnival of the Animals* is an example of legato. You could play a game of Statues with the children, alternating between the two pieces.

More Curriculum Connectors

 Listening skills are necessary not only in music but in the **language arts** as well.

 Experience with — and awareness of — muscle tension falls under the content area of **science**.

What Else I Did

_____

_____

_____

_____

_____

UNIT 18
Pitch

Art ★ Language Arts ★ Mathematics ★ Music ★ Science ★ Social Studies

Do-Re-Mi

What It Teaches

★ The scale

★ Listening skills

★ Levels in space

What You'll Need

Piano, electronic keyboard, xylophone, or the scale written on a staff (optional)

What to Do

★ Sing the scale to the children (do-re-mi-fa-so-la-ti-do), explaining how each successive note is higher in pitch than the previous one.

★ Have the children sing the scale with you.

★ Sing it again, this time asking the children to place their hands in their laps, raising them a little bit higher with each note you sing (and lowering them if you are also singing the descending scale).

★ Once the children have grasped the concept, challenge them to demonstrate with their whole bodies, beginning close to the floor and getting as close to the ceiling as possible (and the reverse).

How to Ensure Success

This activity is one you'll definitely want to perform with the children until they understand what you're expecting.

Depending on your group, limit their initial experiences to a rising scale only, later exploring it in both directions.

If it's possible to demonstrate the scale on a keyboard or on a written staff, the children will be able to *see* as well as hear the rising and descending pitches.

What Else You Can Do

★ Vary this activity to also explore other concepts. The simplest variation is to change the tempo at which you sing the scale.

★ Alternately sing or play in staccato or legato style.

★ Add the concepts of crescendo and decrescendo by beginning at either a soft or loud volume and gradually increasing or decreasing it.

★ Eventually, if the children have become very familiar with the notes of the scale and you have a keyboard or xylophone available, play the notes out of order, challenging the children to demonstrate with their arms or whole bodies whether a note was higher or lower than the previous one.

More Curriculum Connectors

 The concept of levels in space is also relative to **art** and **mathematics**.

 Listening skills are a part of **language arts**.

What Else I Did

_____

_____

_____

_____

_____

High and Low

What It Teaches

★ Pitch identification

★ Levels in space

★ Listening skills

What You'll Need

Penny whistle; scarves or streamers (both optional)

What to Do

★ Make a humming sound that goes from a low pitch to a high one and back again (or play the penny whistle).

★ This time, making either low or high humming sounds, ask the children to tell you which is high and which is low. Can they show you high and low with their bodies?

★ Ask the children to crouch low to the floor, raising and lowering their bodies with your rising or descending pitch. Start off by changing your pitch slowly, increasing your tempo each time you repeat it. The faster you get, the more hilarious the children will think it is!

How to Ensure Success

If necessary, participate with the children until they grasp the concept.

Begin with arms alone, before asking them to raise and lower their whole bodies.

What Else You Can Do

★ To make the activity more challenging, instead of moving steadily from a low to a high tone or the reverse, hum different pitches, in no particular order, asking the children to show you with their bodies whether the one you're humming is lower or higher than the previous one.

★ Provide each child with a scarf or a streamer and challenge them to move the prop at a high level when they hear a high pitch and at a low level when they hear a low pitch. Can they find different ways to move the prop?

More Curriculum Connectors

Levels in space are a concept in both **art** and **mathematics**.

Listening is one of the four components of **language arts**.

What Else I Did

_____

_____

_____

_____

_____

Moving High/Moving Low

What It Teaches

★   Pitch identification

★   Levels and pathways

★   Listening skills

★   Problem solving

What You'll Need

Piano, electronic keyboard, xylophone, or other instrument(s) on which to play high and low notes; scarves or streamers (optional)

What to Do

★   With the children sitting and listening, demonstrate both high and low notes with your instrument. Ask them to close their eyes and identify which notes you play are high and which are low.

★   Continue the process, this time asking the children to move about the room, finding a way to move at a low level when they hear low notes and moving at a high level when they hear high notes.

How to Ensure Success

Before conducting this activity with the accompanying sound, ask the children to think of and demonstrate some ways to move at both low and high levels. Be sure you get — and enthusiastically point out — a wide variety of responses. (Possibilities for moving at a low level include crawling, creeping, rolling, duck-walking, etc. Possibilities for moving at a high level include walking straight and tall, tiptoeing, jumping, and hopping.)

What Else You Can Do

★   Provide each child with a scarf or streamer and ask them to move the prop at a high or low level as they move around the room.

★   For more of a challenge, ask the children to move the prop at the same level at which they themselves are moving (coinciding with the pitch of the notes played). For example, if they're moving at a high level, they must also be moving the prop at a high level. If they're rolling or duck-walking, for instance, they must simultaneously move the prop at a low level.

★   Ask the children to take partners and to find a way to move at high and low levels while connected to each other (e.g., holding hands, arms linked, etc.).

More Curriculum Connectors

 Levels and pathways are a part of both **mathematics** and **art**.

 Listening skills are as essential to **language arts** as they are to music.

 The cooperation required in the partner activity falls under the heading of **social studies**.

What Else I Did

_____

_____

_____

_____

_____

Mood

Art ★ Language Arts ★ Mathematics ★ Music ★ Science ★ Social Studies

In a Mellow Mood

What It Teaches

★ Association of music and mood

★ Self-awareness

★ Focused listening

★ Relaxation

What You'll Need

A recording of a piece of music suitable for relaxation or "quiet times" (possibilities include "Quiet Times" and "Classical Quiet Times" by Rae Pica and Richard Gardzina (two of the six cassettes in *More Music for Moving & Learning*), Hap Palmer's *Quiet Places* and *Sea Gulls,* and Joanie Bartels' *Lullaby Magic I, Lullaby Magic II,* and *Quiet Moments with Greg and Steve*)

What to Do

★ Play — at a reasonably low volume — the piece of music you've chosen for the children.

★ Ask the children to tell you what it brings to mind.

★ Challenge them to show you with their bodies what it makes them think of.

How to Ensure Success

If the children need encouragement, you can use words such as *soothing, gentle, calm,* or *easy* to get the idea across.

Of course, even if a child responds in an "energetic" way, acknowledge and validate the child's right to feel that way.

What Else You Can Do

★ Suggest specific relaxation techniques as quiet music plays in the background. For instance, encourage the children to pretend to melt, to be balloons inflating and deflating (slowly inhaling and exhaling), or to be statues and rag dolls (alternately tightening and relaxing muscles).

More Curriculum Connectors

 Relaxation falls under the heading of **science**.

 Self-awareness is the beginning of **social studies** for young children.

 Focused listening is also a component of **language arts**.

What Else I Did

_____

_____

_____

_____

_____

What Mood Are You In?

What It Teaches

★   Awareness and expression of emotions

★   Association of feelings with the moods depicted by music

★   Focused listening

What You'll Need

Two recordings — one you consider to be a very "happy" piece (e.g., Beethoven's "Ode to Joy" or Scott Joplin's "The Entertainer") and one that feels very "sad" to you (e.g., Samuel Barber's "Adagio for Strings" or a funeral march)

What to Do

★   Ask the children to show you how they move when feeling happy. Challenge them to demonstrate how they move differently when feeling really sad.

★   Play the song you've chosen for "happy," asking the children to show you their happy movements as it's playing. Repeat with the "sad" song.

★   Alternate between the two, not indicating which is which and challenging them to simply move in either a happy or sad way, depending on how the music makes them feel.

How to Ensure Success

Ask the children for actual examples of times they felt really happy and others when they felt really sad. What made them feel that way? How did their bodies look and move each time?

What Else You Can Do

★   Choose pieces of music that demonstrate other feelings children can relate to — scared (e.g., an eerie piece of electronic music), proud (e.g., a patriotic march), or silly (e.g., "Baby Elephant Walk," "Syncopated Clock," or "Itsy Bitsy Teeny Weeny Yellow Polka Dot Bikini"). Use the preceding process to explore each of these.

More Curriculum Connectors

 Awareness and expression of feelings is an important first step in **social studies**.

 Discussing feelings and the situations that cause them constitutes **language arts**.

What Else I Did

_____

_____

_____

_____

_____

In the Mood

What It Teaches

★ Awareness and expression of emotions

★ Recognition of the moods expressed by music

★ Listening skills

What You'll Need

A selection of recordings depicting different moods the children can relate to, such as happy, sad, proud, tired, scared, silly, or mad (possibilities include *Patriotic Songs of the USA,* available from Melody House, for proud; Bach's "Musette in D-Major" for happy; Brahms' "Lullaby" for tired; and the theme music from a science fiction movie for scared); a selection of instruments and/or props (optional)

What to Do

★ Play one of the pieces you've chosen and ask the children to move in whatever way they'd like to move to it. After a while, repeat with another selection.

★ Repeat this process, playing the pieces in a random order, always asking the children to move in a way the music makes them want to move.

How to Ensure Success

Children are often more sensitive to the feelings conveyed by music than adults are, so they may not necessarily have the same reaction to a piece of music that you do. They may even respond differently from *each other*! That's fine; the idea is for them to react to the music in whatever way it makes *them* feel. Let them know it's acceptable for them to respond individually.

What Else You Can Do

★ Play a game of Statues, using a variety of pieces with different moods, and ask the children to freeze in a statue pose that represents the mood they're portraying.

★ Have a variety of musical instruments and/or props available for the children to choose from (multiple numbers of each). When a particular piece of music is played, each child selects an instrument or a prop to use that she or he finds most suitable for the mood of the music.

More Curriculum Connectors

 Awareness and expression of emotion are part of **social studies**.

 The focused listening required is also an element of **language arts**.

What Else I Did

_____

_____

_____

_____

_____

Rhythm

Art ★ Language Arts ★ Mathematics ★ Music ★ Science ★ Social Studies

Body Rhythm

What It Teaches

★ An introduction to rhythm

★ Problem solving

What You'll Need

No equipment needed

What to Do

★ Challenge the children to discover how many sounds they can create with their hands.

★ What other body parts can they use to create sound? (Possibilities include feet, tongue, and teeth.)

★ Ask them to move around the room, accompanying themselves with some of these sounds. Can they use different parts of the room (floor, walls, chalk-board) to create new sounds?

How to Ensure Success

Children love to make noise, and making noise with their bodies is a great introduction to rhythm. You may have to reassure them, however, that it's really fine for them to be making noise.

You can perhaps encourage the creation of new and different sounds by suggesting such words as *clap, stamp, stomp, flick, scuff, shuffle,* or *pat.*

What Else You Can Do

★ Talk to the children about the sounds of a cough, sneeze, yawn, hiccup, giggle, and snore. Ask them to show you how each sound makes their bodies move. Ask them to either incorporate the sound into their movements or to perform silently. Challenge them to perform each movement more than once.

More Curriculum Connectors

 Investigating the possibilities for moving and creating sounds with different body parts is a great **science** experiment for young children.

 The concept of *how many* falls under the heading of **mathematics**.

 Attaching meaning to the words in the extension activity incorporates **language arts**.

What Else I Did

_____

_____

_____

_____

_____

Match the Movement

What It Teaches

★ Awareness of rhythm

★ Listening skills

What You'll Need

Hand drum and mallet or appropriate substitutes (e.g., a coffee can with a plastic lid and a wooden spoon)

What to Do

★ Ask the children to walk around the room in any way they like.

★ With your drum, beat out a rhythmic pattern that matches their movements. When they change their movements (for example, from small to big steps or from light to heavy ones), change the drumbeat to match those movements.

★ Repeat the process with other locomotor skills (running, galloping, jumping, etc.).

How to Ensure Success

Very young children aren't developmentally ready to match their movements to an imposed beat. Synchronizing your instrumental accompaniment to *their* rhythm automatically sets them up for success. They love realizing they're responsible for the rhythms you're creating!

If the children don't vary their movements on their own, suggest that they change their tempo, force, or pathways.

What Else You Can Do

★ The children also love it when you let the drum dictate the kind of movement they should perform. For instance, swish the mallet quietly around the drum-skin to inspire soft movements or beat the drum loudly and slowly for giant steps. You can tap the side of the drum with the stick itself to inspire light, percussive movement. (Be sure, however, that you're not expecting the children to be able to move "at one" with the beat.)

★ With just a little bit of experience with the preceding game, the children can take responsibility for the instrumental accompaniment. Give each child a turn to control the drum and watch their eyes light up as they realize the power they have in their hands!

More Curriculum Connectors

 Listening skills are also a component of **language arts**.

 If possible, use a variety of percussion instruments originating from different parts of the world to contribute to the children's multicultural education (**social studies**).

What Else I Did

_____

_____

_____

_____

_____

Echo

What It Teaches

★ An introduction to beat groupings (meters)

★ Counting

★ Listening skills

What You'll Need

No equipment needed

What to Do

★ Explain to the children that you're going to clap a certain number of times and, after you've finished, you want them to clap, too — to echo what they heard you do.

★ Clap and count out a small group of beats (e.g., 1–2 or 1–2–3).

★ Continue the process, clapping and counting, with the children echoing you.

How to Ensure Success

When you first perform this activity, it's a good idea to repeat each beat grouping at least once to give children a second chance to hear it and repeat it successfully.

Start with a very small number of beats, not exceeding four to begin.

Clap and count at a slow to moderate tempo until your children are ready for a faster pace.

What Else You Can Do

★ To create variety, repeat or "mix and match" groupings. For example, clap and count 1–2, 1–2, or try something like 1–2, 1–2–3.

★ To make the game more challenging, clap without counting aloud.

★ Once the children are comfortable clapping various beat groupings, ask them to stand and try stepping in place to each beat. You may have to return to a slower tempo for a while.

More Curriculum Connectors

 Counting, of course, is a part of **mathematics**.

 Listening is one of the components of **language arts**.

Ask the children in your class for whom English is a second language to teach everyone how to count to four in their first language (**social studies**).

What Else I Did

_____

_____

_____

_____

_____

Common Meters

What It Teaches

★   An introduction to meters commonly used in Western music

★   Appreciation for a variety of music

★   Listening skills

★   Practice with various movement skills

What You'll Need

Recordings of music in 2/4, 3/4, and 4/4 meters; recordings in a 6/8, 5/4, 5/8, or 7/8 meter (optional)

What to Do

★   Choose a piece of music with a 2/4 meter (for example, a march or a polka) and play a little bit of it for the children to hear.

★   Start the piece again and encourage the children to try your suggested movements to accompany it. Possibilities for 2/4 include clapping 1–2, marching, stamping feet, jumping, and hopping.

★   Repeat the process with a piece in 3/4 (a waltz is most common). Suggested movements might include clapping 1–2–3, swaying, and swinging bodies or body parts (e.g., arms, legs, head).

★   Repeat the process with a piece in a 4/4 meter (rock and roll and many Top 40 songs are performed in this most common meter). Movement possibilities include clapping 1–2–3–4, jogging, stamping feet, and bouncing up and down.

How to Ensure Success

Depending on the developmental level of the children and the amount of time available, extend these activities over a period of days, perhaps concentrating on one meter per session.

Choose to have the children simply move in any way they want to each meter before asking them to try your suggestions.

Perform the suggested movements with the children at first.

What Else You Can Do

★   For more of a challenge, explore a 6/8 meter (six eighth-notes to the measure, found often in folk songs and some marches). Movement possibilities include clapping 1–2, marching, rocking, and moving the head from side to side.

★   Also challenging are pieces in meters less common to the United States, like 5/4, 5/8, and 7/8. Invite the children to move in any way they want to these pieces.

★   Play a game of Statues, alternating between each of these meters.

More Curriculum Connectors

 Listening skills are also necessary to **language arts**.

 Using pieces representative of different ethnicities contributes to multicultural education, which falls under the heading of **social studies**.

 If you count claps you'll be incorporating an aspect of **mathematics**.

What Else I Did

_____

_____

_____

_____

_____

SCIENCE

Art ★ Language Arts ★ Mathematics ★ Music ★ Science ★ Social Studies

The word *science* reminds many adults of such topics as chemistry, physics, biology, botany, and astronomy. We might imagine men and women in laboratory coats, poring over facts and figures or measuring strange concoctions into test tubes and beakers. Since none of this is relevant in the lives of young children, you might wonder — rightly — how science fits into the early childhood curriculum.

The fact is, science is also about exploration, investigation, problem solving, and discovery — all of which *are* relevant for young children. A child's whole life, from its very beginning, is exploring, investigating, solving problems, and discovering!

The principal difference between these two views of science is that much of the former deals with the theoretical and the abstract, while the latter, as far as young children are concerned, deals with the concrete and the tangible — with what can be readily observed. For example, children discover which objects will float or sink by actually placing objects in water. They discover a different type of floating by blowing bubbles through a wand and watching them drift through the air. Balls, however, will not float when sent into the air; this is due to gravity, a concept the children may not grasp but one they can witness firsthand.

In other words, science for young children is learning by doing — just as movement is.

Many themes typically explored in classrooms and child care centers fall in the science category, including such themes as the human body (body parts and their functions, hygiene, and nutrition), seasons, and animals. These are covered in the lesson plans that follow, as are specific scientific concepts appropriate for exploration with young children.

Of course, any time children perform movements — locomotor, nonlocomotor, manipulative, gymnastic, or dance — they are learning something about the functions of the human body. It could be said, therefore, that whenever children are moving, they're also learning something about science!

UNIT 21

My Body

Simon Says

What It Teaches

★ Body part identification

★ Listening skills

What You'll Need

No equipment needed

What to Do

★ Arrange the children into two groups — either in circles or lines.

★ Explain that you're going to pretend to be someone called "Simon," and when you say "Simon says…," they're to do whatever Simon has asked them to do. But if you tell them to do something without first saying "Simon says," they shouldn't do it! If they do, they should move from the line or circle they're in to the other one.

★ "Simon's" commands can include such challenges as touching different body parts (toes, shoulders, elbows, etc.), blinking eyes, wiggling fingers or noses, waving hands, puckering lips, bending knees, standing on one foot, and giving themselves a hug.

How to Ensure Success

If your children are too young to grasp the concept of Simon, use the name of a favorite stuffed animal or character.

Performing the action with the children at first almost guarantees success, because people have been shown to respond better to visual signals than audible signals.

Eliminating the elimination process pretty much ensures the children won't feel badly about moving without Simon having said they could. Just make sure they realize that moving from one group to the other is part of the fun, too!

What Else You Can Do

★ Another option is simply to play a game called "Show Me," in which you call out various body parts and actions you want the children to display. These games can't be repeated too often! Not only is body part identification an important first step in movement and physical education, but once children enter elementary school they won't have many opportunities to partake in such self-awareness activities.

★ Other body part activities include "Heads, Bellies, Toes" and "Head, Shoulders, Knees, and Toes."

More Curriculum Connectors

  Listening skills are essential to both **language arts** and **music**.

Self-awareness is also the first step in **social studies** for young children. You can include a multicultural element by saying the body parts in different languages. Do any of your children know the words for these body parts in another language?

What Else I Did

_____

_____

_____

_____

_____

Hands Down

What It Teaches

★ Body awareness

★ Self-expression

What You'll Need

No equipment needed

What to Do

★ Have a discussion with the children about their hands. What are the different parts that make up a hand? Have they ever thought about all the things their hands do for them?

★ Ask them to pretend to do a variety of things with their hands and to think about the many ways they have to move their hands to accomplish these tasks. Possible challenges include pretending to wave hello or goodbye, play the piano or guitar, brush teeth, brush hair, wash the face, button clothes, pull up a zipper, bounce a ball, dial a phone, tie shoes, and turn the pages of a book.

How to Ensure Success

There is no wrong way to respond here, but if it makes the children more comfortable, demonstrate the activities when you first begin playing this game.

Using only challenges the children can relate to — given their age and experience — will also ensure success. For instance, a preschooler in New York City might be able to demonstrate hailing a cab, but a child raised in the suburbs or the country would be completely unfamiliar with this action.

What Else You Can Do

★ Play a game of "Feet First," in which you ask the children to demonstrate all the possible things feet can do. Possibilities include walking, climbing stairs or ladders, jogging, jumping, hopping, tiptoeing, ice skating, and kicking a ball. This is a great way to get them moving!

More Curriculum Connectors

 Self-awareness and self-expression are also components of **social studies**.

 Read *Here Are My Hands* by Bill Martin, Jr. and John Archambault or *The Soles of Your Feet* by Genichiro Yagyu to incorporate **language arts**.

What Else I Did

_____

_____

_____

_____

_____

Move It!

What It Teaches

★   Body awareness

★   Practice with motor skills

★   Listening skills

What You'll Need

No equipment needed

What to Do

★   Tell the children you're going to call out one way of moving after another and they're to move that way until they hear you say "Freeze."

★   Call out different locomotor skills — walk, run, jump, leap, gallop, hop, slide, and skip — varying the amount of time you have them move and freeze.

How to Ensure Success

Only call out those skills you're sure all of the children can execute.

Let the children dictate the length of this game. If you see them begin to tire, bring the game to an end.

What Else You Can Do

★   Once the children are able to perform many locomotor skills well on their own, play a "numbers" game. Challenge the children to perform each skill as you call it out, as before. But when they hear you call out a number, they must connect to enough other children to make up that number and continue performing the skill. In other words, if they were galloping and you called out the number three, they would each have to find two other children, make a connection of some kind (hands held, elbows linked, etc.), and continue galloping.

★   Play the original game with nonlocomotor skills — bend, stretch, sit, shake, turn, rock, sway, swing, and twist — challenging the children to find many different ways of performing each skill.

★   When your children are developmentally ready, call out *combinations* of skills, beginning with two at a time. For example, you might challenge them to perform two different locomotor skills, one after the other (e.g., walk–jump), or you could combine a locomotor with a nonlocomotor skill (e.g., walk–stretch).

More Curriculum Connectors

  Listening skills are linked to both **language arts** and **music**. You can incorporate more music by using movement-inspiring albums such as *Mr. Al Sings and Moves* or Rae Pica's *Let's Move & Learn*.

 Performing locomotor skills while "connected" to others is a cooperative activity and thus falls under the category of **social studies**.

Having to count the number of children with whom they connect — or the number of ways you can perform each nonlocomotor skill — constitutes **mathematics**.

What Else I Did

_____

_____

_____

_____

_____

Common Senses

What It Teaches

★ Self-awareness

★ Identification of and appreciation for the various senses

★ Self-expression

What You'll Need

No equipment needed

What to Do

★ Talk to the children about the things they like most to taste, smell, hear, feel, and see. What things do they like least?

★ Using some of their responses, ask them now to show you how their faces and/or bodies move in reaction to these tastes, smells, sounds, textures, and sights. For example, what happens when they taste a sour lemon, a very bubbly drink, peanut butter, or their favorite ice cream; smell a skunk, cookies baking, onions, or flowers; hear a very loud noise or their favorite music; have on a "scratchy" sweater, feel their pet's fur, or accidentally touch something hot; or look for something lost on the floor or look up at the stars at night.

How to Ensure Success

If you feel exploring all this territory at one time will be overwhelming for the children, focus on one sense per session.

If the children need extra "coaching," use descriptive words to help them respond. For example, ask if a sour lemon makes them feel like puckering up their mouths or if they describe the scratchy sweater as being very itchy or pinchy.

What Else You Can Do

★ The listening activities in the Language Arts section would fit in with your exploration of the sense of hearing.

★ Ask the children to depict the shape or movement of some of the sources of these tastes, smells, sounds, textures, and sights (e.g., a bubbly drink, a skunk, or a hot iron).

More Curriculum Connectors

 Self-awareness is part of **social studies**.

 Texture is a component of **art**, as is the ability to translate what one sees into another means of expression.

What Else I Did

_____

_____

_____

_____

_____

A Breath of Fresh Air

What It Teaches

★   Relaxation

★   Proper breathing

★   Self-control

★   Contraction and release of the muscles

What You'll Need

No equipment needed

What to Do

★   Talk to the children about balloons and what's meant by inflating and deflating. Do inflation and deflation happen quickly or slowly?

★   Ask them to imagine they're each a balloon — in whatever color they choose. Have the children pretend to "inflate" by inhaling and then "deflate" by exhaling — slowly!

★   Repeat the activity a couple of times until the children have achieved a certain level of relaxation.

How to Ensure Success

Demonstrating inflation and deflation with an actual balloon helps make the image more vivid.

Before "inflating," ask them to start off in a small shape, as close to the floor as possible. They're then going to get bigger, just as balloons do when inflating. While deflating, they should get smaller and smaller, just as balloons do.

Be sure they inhale and exhale through their noses by explaining that's the opening through which the air is going to come in and go out.

What Else You Can Do

★   To inspire relaxation through contraction and release of the muscles, play Statues/Rag Dolls. For this activity, ask them first to look like a statue (explain that statues are very stiff). Then ask them to show you what a rag doll looks like. Alternate between the two images, finishing with the rag doll.

★ "Melting" is a wonderful slow-motion activity that helps the children unwind. Talk to them about how slowly ice cream cones, snow sculptures, or ice cubes melt. Ask them to stand and demonstrate one of these possibilities.

More Curriculum Connectors

 Because **music** is mood-altering, it offers wonderful possibilities for relaxation. Accompany any of these activities with pieces recorded especially for resting and quiet times (there are many children's albums written just for this purpose) or with classical or New Age compositions you've found to be very soothing.

 The quantitative concepts of *bigger* and *smaller* fall under the heading of **mathematics**.

 Read Genichiro Yagyu's *The Holes in Your Nose* to incorporate **language arts**.

What Else I Did

_____

_____

_____

_____

_____

UNIT 22

Hygiene

Art ★ Language Arts ★ Mathematics ★ Music ★ Science ★ Social Studies

Rub-a-Dub-Dub

What It Teaches

★ Cleanliness can be fun

★ Body part identification

What You'll Need

No equipment needed

What to Do

★ Talk to the children about washing up. What are the times when they should always wash their hands (e.g., after going to the bathroom or after coughing or sneezing)? Why is it important? What is their favorite color washcloth at home? Do they have special toys they take into the tub with them? What kind of soap do they use?

★ Ask them to show you how they would wash various body parts, like the face, hands, elbows, knees, tummy, back, neck, and feet. Stress realism.

★ Accompany the activity with the nursery rhyme "Rub-a-Dub-Dub," substituting the word "kids" for "men." Or, to the melody of "The Mulberry Bush," sing "This is the way we wash our [hands] . . ."

How to Ensure Success

There's no way to get this activity wrong! Be sure you ask the children to wash parts you know they can readily identify.

What Else You Can Do

★ When the children are ready, make the activity more challenging by including such body parts as wrists, shins, throat, and temples.

★ Introduce — or give the children greater experience with — laterality by asking them to "wash" parts on just one side of the body. For example, you could challenge them to wash the *left* knee or the *right* foot.

More Curriculum Connectors

 Using the nursery rhyme involves **language arts**, while using the song will include both language arts and **music**.

What Else I Did

_____

_____

_____

_____

_____

Hair Care

What It Teaches

★ The various aspects of hair care

What You'll Need

No equipment needed

What to Do

★ Talk to the children about the following aspects of hair care. What's their favorite shampoo? Do they brush or comb their hair? How many in the room have long hair and how many have short hair? Are there children who wear their hair in braids, plaits, or beaded?

★ Ask the children to demonstrate the motions involved in any or all of the above hair-related tasks.

★ Challenge them to pretend to be the following: shampoo bubbling, a comb or brush running down a long mane of hair, running water, scissors cutting hair, and a blow dryer.

How to Ensure Success

Expect as many responses to your challenges as there are children. You'll be amazed at how many different ways they can find to "be" water, for example.

What Else You Can Do

★ Ask the children to show you all the things hairstylists and barbers might do in their work. (Offer verbal assistance if they get stuck.)

More Curriculum Connectors

 Counting the number of children with short and long hair constitutes **mathematics**.

 Pretending to be hairstylists and barbers is an exploration of occupations, which falls under the heading of **social studies**.

What Else I Did

_____

_____

_____

_____

_____

A Bite Out of Life

What It Teaches

★ Appreciation of dental care

What You'll Need

Toothbrush, floss, toothpaste, etc., or pictures of them (optional)

What to Do

★ Discuss dental care with the children. What colors are their toothbrushes at home? What's their favorite toothpaste? How many times a day do they brush? Do they know what flossing is?

★ Ask them to demonstrate the following possibilities: the shape of a toothbrush, the motion of a battery-powered toothbrush, the shape of a piece of floss (how long can they make themselves?), the motion of floss sliding between the teeth, how wide they can open their mouths, toothpaste coming out of the tube, the toothpaste tube being squeezed, and the toothpaste tube being rolled up from the bottom.

How to Ensure Success

Having the preceding items (or pictures of them) available for the children to see can help them more accurately portray those items.

When necessary, use verbal encouragement. For example, tell the children a battery-powered toothbrush *vibrates,* which is like very fast shaking.

What Else You Can Do

★ Challenge the children to discover how many different sounds they can create with their teeth and then accompany their sounds with movements. (Explain that their teeth can be like rhythm instruments.)

More Curriculum Connectors

 Taking on various shapes with the body falls under the heading of **art**.

 The creation of sound constitutes **music**. To add more music, play Raffi's "Brush Your Teeth," from *Singable Songs for the Very Young,* and "Brush Away," from Volume II of Hap Palmer's *Learning Basic Skills Through Music.*

 Ask the children to count the different sounds they can make with their teeth to include **mathematics**.

What Else I Did

_____

_____

_____

_____

_____

Laundry Day

What It Teaches

★ Appreciation for clothes care

★ Experience with household machines

What You'll Need

No equipment needed

What to Do

★ Talk to the children about washing machines, dryers, ironing, and other elements of clothes care. Do they know the difference between a gentle cycle and a spin cycle? Does the washing machine at home open from the top or from the front? How about the dryer? Does the dryer have a window in its door so they can watch the clothes go around and around?

★ Challenge the children to demonstrate the actions of a washing machine, including such possibilities as having its lid opened, filling up with water, churning on gentle cycle or spin cycle, and slowing down and coming to a stop.

★ How can they demonstrate clothes being tumbled in a dryer?

How to Ensure Success

Discussing all these elements in advance can help the children more accurately portray the imagery here, but expect them to relate to the images in their own individual ways.

If there are children in your group who might not have a washer and dryer at home, include a discussion of laundromats.

What Else You Can Do

★ Ask the children to show you the shapes of different articles of clothing, for example, a shirt, pants, a sock, scarf, or hat. Introduce the children to the clothing of other cultures, such as a sari or a kilt.

★ Ask the children to reenact the entire process of dirty clothes being tossed into a hamper to being washed, dried, and ironed — either as the person doing the chores or from the clothes' point of view!

More Curriculum Connectors

 Machinery is yet another aspect of **science**.

 Shape is part of the content area of **art**.

 Ask the children to sing "This is the way we [wash] our clothes" (to the tune of "The Mulberry Bush") as they demonstrate their actions to incorporate **music**.

 Including the dress of other cultures incorporates **social studies**.

What Else I Did

_____

_____

_____

_____

_____

Art ★ Language Arts ★ Mathematics ★ Music ★ Science ★ Social Studies

Eat Your Fruits and Veggies

What It Teaches

★   Familiarity with one of the basic food groups

★   The movement element of shape

★   The concept of size

What You'll Need

Various fruits and vegetables or pictures of them

What to Do

★   Talk to the children about various fruits and vegetables, showing pictures of as many as possible. What are their favorite fruits and vegetables? How do they like to eat them? Explain that we're supposed to eat several servings of each every day because they're such an important source of "fuel" for the body.

★   Ask the children to demonstrate the shapes of various fruits and vegetables with their bodies or body parts. Possibilities include bananas, grapes, oranges, pumpkins (doing these three consecutively helps them consider the concept of size), pears, zucchini or squash, and carrots.

How to Ensure Success

Having pictures — or the actual fruits and vegetables — available will greatly contribute to both the discussion and demonstration.

Be sure to talk about how some foods have the same shape (grapes, oranges, and pumpkins, for example) but differ quite a bit in size.

What Else You Can Do

★   Talk to the children about the "before" and "after" of some fruits and vegetables. Ask the children to depict them for you. Possibilities include an apple hanging on a tree/applesauce simmering on the stove, a grape/grape jelly being spread, an orange being peeled/orange juice being poured, or a potato being peeled/a potato being mashed. (If possible, actually *prepare* some fruits and vegetables so the children can get tangible evidence of raw versus cooked. Then have a tasting party!)

More Curriculum Connectors

 The element of shape is a major factor in **art**.

 The concept of size is part of **mathematics**.

 Cathy Slonecki's album *Eat Well! Feel Well!* (available from Educational Activities) is dedicated to nutrition and includes such songs as "The Vegetable Rock" (**music**).

 Read *Oliver's Vegetables* by Vivian French to incorporate **language arts**.

What Else I Did

_____

_____

_____

_____

_____

Get Ready, Spaghetti!

What It Teaches

★   Awareness of a component of the food group from which we're to eat the most servings

★   The movement element of force

★   The movement element of shape

What You'll Need

A variety of pastas in different shapes; rice (both optional)

What to Do

★   Talk to the children about spaghetti. What shape is it? What is it like when it's uncooked? What happens when it's placed in boiling water? What happens if cooked spaghetti is left on the plate too long? Is it hard or soft then? What shape is it then?

★   Challenge the children to portray spaghetti in its various stages: uncooked and in a box, coming out of the box, being placed in boiling water, being stirred, being placed on a plate, and being left out and drying up.

How to Ensure Success

Being as specific as possible in your discussion will contribute to the success of this venture.

If possible, actually cooking spaghetti in the classroom prior to participating in these activities will contribute greatly to the children's understanding and knowledge.

As the children are depicting the various stages, you may need to provide additional verbal help. For example, you might want to use words like *stiff, loose, limp,* or *hard.*

What Else You Can Do

★   Talk about — or display — pastas of varying shapes (e.g., rotini or spiral, bowtie, shells, lasagna, ravioli). Challenge the children to show you these different shapes with their bodies.

★ Rice is another component of this food group and is eaten throughout the world. Talk to the children about rice in its precooked and cooked states (demonstrate if possible) and invite them to depict the transformation from small, hard morsels to soft, plumped rice. Be sure they understand this is a *slow* process.

More Curriculum Connectors

 The movement element of force involves muscle tension, which is yet another aspect of **science**.

 The movement element of shape is a component of **art**.

 The discussion regarding spaghetti constitutes **language arts**.

 Everybody Cooks Rice by Norah Dooley offers another **language arts** component as well as **social studies**, because the main character roams her neighborhood and discovers different families, from different countries, all cooking with rice.

 The measuring involved in cooking pasta and/or rice falls under the heading of **mathematics**.

What Else I Did

_____

_____

_____

_____

_____

Bread, Bread, Bread

What It Teaches

★ Awareness of another component of the food group from which we're to eat the most servings

What You'll Need

No equipment needed

What to Do

★ Talk to the children about bread making *before* the advent of bread machines, reviewing the various steps involved (stirring the ingredients to make the dough and then kneading, rolling, shaping, and baking the dough).

★ To the tune of "The Mulberry Bush," sing "This is the way we stir (knead, roll, shape, bake) the dough," accompanying each verse with the appropriate motions.

How to Ensure Success

During the discussion, be sure the children fully understand the concepts involved.

If necessary, perform the actions with the children at first.

If possible, make bread in the classroom.

What Else You Can Do

★ Challenge the children to demonstrate what it would be like to *be* the dough as it's stirred, kneaded, rolled out, shaped, and baked. (What happens when it's baked? Answer: It rises some more and becomes more firm.)

★ Ask the children to show you the shapes of their favorite types of breads. These might include such breads as muffins, pretzels, or bagels.

More Curriculum Connectors

 Accompanying the children's actions with a song incorporates **music** into the lesson, while the creation of new lyrics constitutes **language arts**.

 To further incorporate **language arts**, read *Bread, Bread, Bread* by Ann Morris and/or *Everybody Bakes Bread* by Norah Dooley. Both of these books are multicultural in nature (**social studies**).

 Exploring the shapes of various breads falls under the heading of **art**.

What Else I Did

_____

_____

_____

_____

_____

The Great Pyramid

What It Teaches

★ An introduction to the basic food groups and their relationship to one another

★ The movement element of shape

What You'll Need

A picture of the food pyramid

What to Do

★ Talk to the children about the food pyramid. What geometric shape is like a pyramid? How many points does it have? Demonstrate how it starts off wide at the bottom and gradually narrows to a point. Explain that the foods at the bottom are the ones from which we should have the most servings daily, with each succeeding group requiring fewer servings.

★ Challenge the children to show you the shape of a pyramid with their bodies or body parts.

How to Ensure Success

Having a picture of a pyramid (or even a triangle) will contribute greatly.

Having the option of creating the pyramid with either the whole body or with body parts will help. Certain body parts, like the hands and the legs, are easier to make triangles with.

What Else You Can Do

★ Challenge groups of four to create the shape of a pyramid together, each representing a different level or food group. (This is not meant to be the kind of pyramid cheerleaders make.)

More Curriculum Connectors

 The movement element of shape is a component of **art**, while the concept of a triangle, specifically, falls under the heading of **mathematics**.

 The cooperation involved in the alternate activity constitutes **social studies**.

What Else I Did

_____

_____

_____

_____

_____

UNIT 24
Seasons

Autumn

What It Teaches

★ Awareness of the fall season as experienced in many parts of the country

★ Awareness of weather concepts

★ The movement element of force

What You'll Need

Parachute and cut out (or real) leaves (optional)

What to Do

★ Talk to the children about how the leaves change colors and then fall from the trees during autumn in many parts of the country. How do they fall — heavily, hitting the ground with a lot of force, or lightly, taking a while to gently descend to earth?

★ Also ask them to tell you how the weather changes. Does it get warmer or colder in the fall? What's the wind like in autumn?

★ Invite the children to depict leaves falling from the trees. You act as the wind, "blowing them around." Challenge them to "fly" higher and lower and to spin and swirl.

How to Ensure Success

Encourage the children to move as lightly as possible by using words such as *gentle, easy,* and *drifting.*

What Else You Can Do

★ Scatter cut out, colored leaves (or actual fallen leaves) on a parachute being held by the children. How can the children make the leaves "fall to the ground?"

★ Challenge the children to demonstrate the actions involved in certain autumn activities, like raking leaves and then jumping in the pile. How would picking apples look different from picking pumpkins?

More Curriculum Connectors

 The movement element of force involves muscle tension, which is another aspect of **science**, as is the concept of cause and effect (between the wind and the leaves).

 Positional concepts like *higher* and *lower* fall under the headings of both **art** and **mathematics**.

 Read the book *Leaves* by Fulvio Testa (with English text by Naomi Lewis) to incorporate **language arts**.

What Else I Did

_____

_____

_____

_____

_____

Winter

What It Teaches

★ Awareness of the winter season as experienced in many parts of the country

★ Familiarity with the concepts of small and large and the gradations in between

★ The movement element of time

★ Experience with relaxation

What You'll Need

A large thermometer; parachute and cotton balls (both optional)

What to Do

★ Talk to the children about building snowpeople. Have they ever made one? Discuss the fact that they start with a single snowball and then gradually increase the snowball in size.

★ Challenge the children to show you what they would look like if they were each a snowball. Ask them to imagine they're being built into snowpeople, gradually getting bigger and bigger.

★ When the "snowpeople" are as big as they can get, ask them to imagine the sun is shining on them, causing them to slowly melt — until they're nothing but puddles on the ground.

How to Ensure Success

Because moving very slowly doesn't come naturally to most children, encourage them to do so — both when they're growing and when melting.

What Else You Can Do

★ When the children are ready to work in partners, they can take turns shaping each other into "snow sculptures."

★ Ask the children to demonstrate what their hands do when they're very cold. How do their bodies look? Ask them to show you how they shiver — just a little and then very hard.

★ Invite the children to demonstrate the actions involved in a variety of winter sports. Possibilities include skating, cross-country skiing, downhill skiing, playing hockey, and snowshoeing.

★ Talk to the children about falling temperatures in the winter. Show them a thermometer, explaining that the mercury falls as the temperature does. Challenge them to pretend they're mercury at the warmest point in the day. At what level would they be? As the sun sets and the temperature drops, so does the mercury. How can they demonstrate that? Would the movement be fast or slow?

★ Place several handfuls of cotton balls or styrofoam peanuts on a parachute, challenging the children to create a "snowstorm."

More Curriculum Connectors

 The concept of size is part of **mathematics**.

 The cooperation involved in the partner activity constitutes **social studies**.

 The partner activity also involves the element of shape, which is part of **art**.

 To incorporate **language arts**, read Anne and Harlow Rockwell's *The First Snowfall* or Allen Morgan's *Sadie and the Snowman*.

What Else I Did

_____

_____

_____

_____

_____

Spring

What It Teaches

★ Awareness of the spring season as experienced in many parts of the country

★ Awareness of the cycle of life

★ The movement element of time

★ The concept of size

What You'll Need

No equipment needed

What to Do

★ Talk to the children about the planting of seeds in the spring. What happens as the weather warms up and the ground (seeds) receives both rain and sunshine? Do the resulting flowers and plants grow quickly or slowly?

★ Invite the children to imagine they're tiny seeds under the earth. With you alternately acting as the sun and the rain, the "seeds" begin to slowly grow into beautiful plants and flowers.

★ What would the plants and flowers look like if a warm spring breeze were blowing them? What if there was a lot of rain and it made the plants and flowers "droopy"?

How to Ensure Success

Encourage the children to grow as slowly as possible by reminding them that it takes a long time for seeds to become plants and flowers.

What Else You Can Do

★ Spring cleaning is as much a part of the season as any climate changes. Talk to the children about spring cleaning and then ask them to demonstrate the actions involved in the various tasks. Possibilities include washing windows, painting, shampooing the carpet, shaking out rugs, and putting away winter clothes.

More Curriculum Connectors

 The concept of size is relevant to both **art** and **mathematics**.

 Introduce the spring cleaning activity by discussing the work of homemakers and professional housecleaners (or painters), thus initiating a discussion of occupations, which falls under the heading of **social studies**.

 Accompany the principal activity with Eric Carle's *The Tiny Seed* to incorporate **language arts**.

What Else I Did

_____

_____

_____

_____

_____

Summer

What It Teaches

★ Awareness of the summer season

★ Awareness of the rising and setting of the sun

★ Introduction to geographical directions

★ The movement element of time

★ The concepts of up and down

★ Levels in space

What You'll Need

A large thermometer (optional)

What to Do

★ Talk to the children about summer. What do they like best about it? What's the weather like during the summer?

★ Explain, as simply as possible, that one of the things they might notice about summer is how long the days stay light. That means the sun rises earlier in the morning and sets later in the evening. Have they ever watched the sun rise or set?

★ Point out the four different geographical directions to the children, explaining that the sun rises in the east and sets in the west.

★ Ask the children to line up side by side on the side of the room you've designated as the east and to crouch down low, waiting for the time when the sun will rise. At a signal from you, they begin to *slowly* rise up and move across the "sky" (the room), "setting" in the west. Can they depict the sun "shining" as they move?

How to Ensure Success

Encourage the children to move as slowly as possible across the room by reminding them of how many hours it takes the sun to rise in the east and set in the west.

What Else You Can Do

★ Talk to the children about different summer sports and activities. Ask them to demonstrate the actions involved in some of them. Possibilities include swimming, tennis, bicycle riding, roller skating, fishing, going on a picnic, and golfing.

★ Talk to the children about rising temperatures in the summer, showing them a thermometer and explaining how the mercury rises as the temperature does. Invite them to start off very low to the floor, pretending to be the mercury on a very cold morning. As the sun rises and the day warms up, they rise, too.

More Curriculum Connectors

 The positional concepts of *up* and *down* are relevant to both **art** and **mathematics**.

 To include **language arts**, read Aliki's *Those Summers* and/or Nina Crews' *One Hot Summer Day* (also **social studies** because it depicts an African-American girl running, eating, and dancing in the city streets).

What Else I Did

_____

_____

_____

_____

_____

UNIT 25
Animals

Art ★ Language Arts ★ Mathematics ★ Music ★ Science ★ Social Studies

My Favorite Animal

What It Teaches

★   Familiarity with various animals and their movements

★   Empathy (imagining what it's like to be something else)

What You'll Need

No equipment needed

What to Do

★   Ask the children to tell you about their favorite animals. What do they like best about them? What size are they? How do they move?

★   Choose one "favorite" at a time, asking all of the children to depict that particular animal in her or his own way. Continue the process, using all — or as many as possible — of the children's responses.

How to Ensure Success

Different children will have different interpretations of how each animal looks and moves. That's fine — and to be encouraged.

Authenticity isn't necessarily the goal at first. For instance, if someone depicts a cat while moving on two feet, be sure to allow it.

What Else You Can Do

★   When the children are ready to work in pairs, have them choose partners. The first partner depicts the actions of an animal of his or her choice (without making any sounds). The second partner must guess and then imitate the animal himself or herself. The children then reverse roles and continue the process.

More Curriculum Connectors

 Discussing favorite animals and the reasons for the children's choices incorporates **language arts** into the activity. You can also read such books as *Animal ABC's* by The World Wildlife Fund or *Animals Black and White* by Phyllis Limbacher Tildes.

 The cooperation involved in the alternate activity qualifies it as **social studies**, as does the fostering of empathy.

 To involve **music**, choose from the many animal-related children's albums available. Possibilities include *Animal Walks, Walk Like the Animals,* and *Save the Animals, Save the Earth,* all available from Kimbo.

What Else I Did

_____

_____

_____

_____

_____

Rabbits and 'Roos

What It Teaches

★ Familiarity with rabbits and kangaroos

★ Size

★ The movement element of force

★ Experience with the locomotor skill of jumping

★ Empathy

What You'll Need

Pictures of rabbits and kangaroos

What to Do

★ Talk to the children about rabbits and kangaroos, showing them pictures of both, if possible. Which is the bigger and which is the smaller? Which would be the heavier of the two? How do these animals move? Which would jump most heavily?

★ Invite the children to move like rabbits and kangaroos, alternating from one to the other.

★ To vary the experience, challenge them to move in straight, curving, and zigzag pathways and at slower and faster speeds. How high can they make their rabbits and kangaroos jump?

How to Ensure Success

Remind the children that rabbits and kangaroos are very *quiet* animals that usually move soundlessly.

At first, allow the children to interpret each animal's movements in her or his own way, even if that means they're not demonstrating size and weight accurately. Later, as you repeat this activity, use follow-up questions to guide them toward discovery of the size and weight differences.

What Else You Can Do

★ Use other pairs of animals to similarly explore contrasts. For example, Kitty Cats and Dinosaurs also demonstrates contrasts in size and force of movement. The Tortoise and the Hare is excellent for exploring contrasts in the movement element of time.

More Curriculum Connectors

 Size, as well as the quantitative concepts of light and heavy, are part of **mathematics**.

 Empathy is critical to **social studies**.

What Else I Did

_____

_____

_____

_____

_____

Giddy-Up

What It Teaches

★   Familiarity with horses

★   Practice with the locomotor skill of galloping

★   Empathy

What You'll Need

No equipment needed

What to Do

★   Talk to the children about horses. Have they ever ridden one? Have they seen horses in person or on television? What are some colors of horses they've seen? How do they move? Discuss galloping with them.

★   Challenge the children to move like horses, encouraging them to pretend they're in an open field, jumping fences, going up and down steep hills, and stopping for occasional drinks of water.

How to Ensure Success

By asking the children to simply pretend to be horses — rather than telling them to gallop — you ensure the children will all experience success. Those children who can gallop will likely do so, and those who can't will still be able to do what you've asked.

Since some children can learn to gallop through imitation, join in the fun yourself so children can witness the proper way to execute this locomotor skill. Be sure they know you don't require that they do exactly as you're doing.

What Else You Can Do

★   Once all the children in your group can gallop, include an exploration of the element of time in the exercise by discussing the difference between a canter and a gallop (cantering is smoother and slower than galloping). Alternately call out the words "gallop" and "canter," with the children responding accordingly.

More Curriculum Connectors

 Empathy is a component of **social studies**.

 If you accompany this activity with a song with a galloping rhythm (something in a 2/4 meter is most appropriate), you can incorporate **music** into it.

What Else I Did

_____

_____

_____

_____

_____

Creepy-Crawly

What It Teaches

★ Experience with cross-lateral movement

★ Experience with a low level in space

★ Empathy

What You'll Need

No equipment needed

What to Do

★ Ask the children to name some of the animals that move along or very near the ground. (Possibilities include snakes, lizards, chameleons, alligators and crocodiles, and seals.)

★ Invite them either to move like their favorite of the animals they mention or like all of them, one after another, as you call out the name of each.

How to Ensure Success

Authenticity is far less important than the opportunity to experience cross-lateral movement. As long as the children are crawling and creeping, allow them to depict each animal according to their own interpretations.

What Else You Can Do

★ The Snake is an activity requiring a great deal of cooperation. Once the children are developmentally ready to handle the responsibility, it's not only fun but beneficial. The game begins with partners lying on their stomachs, one behind the other. The child in back holds onto the ankles of the child in front, forming a two-person snake. These two-person snakes begin to slither around the room, linking up with each other. The snake continues to grow until all of the children are linked, creating one long snake!

More Curriculum Connectors

 The positional concept of *low* is a component of both **art** and **mathematics**.

 Empathy is a part of **social studies**, as is the cooperation required in the alternate activity.

 You can include **music** by using selections from Jane Murphy's *Insects, Bugs and Squiggly Things,* available from Kimbo.

What Else I Did

_____

_____

_____

_____

_____

Ducks, Cows, Cats, and Dogs

What It Teaches

★ Awareness of various animals and their sounds

★ Experience with cross-lateral movement

★ Sound discrimination

★ Cooperation

★ Empathy

What You'll Need

No equipment needed

What to Do

★ Talk to the children about each of the animals named in the title of this game adapted from Docheff (1992). What sound does each of them make?

★ Explain the rules of the game to the children (as described following).

★ Ask the children to space themselves throughout the room. Whisper the name of one of these animals in each player's ear.

★ Once each child has been assigned an animal, the children all close their eyes and get on hands and knees.

★ At your start signal, the "animals" begin to move, making the appropriate sounds. The object of the game is for like animals to find one another. When they've done so, they stop making their sounds and sit and watch the others who are still trying.

How to Ensure Success

For the youngest children, choose to play with only two or three of the animals cited in the title.

Help the children by letting them know when all of the dogs, for example, have found each other. Once they realize they've successfully reached their goal, they can be an audience to the children still playing.

What Else You Can Do

★   To make this activity more challenging for older children, use all four of the animals (ducks, cows, cats, and dogs). If the group is large enough, add other animals with familiar sounds, like pigs, chickens, or sheep.

More Curriculum Connectors

 Because this is a listening — or sound discrimination — activity, it falls under the headings of **music** and **language arts**.

 Empathy and cooperation qualify the game as **social studies**.

 Once all the "animals" have found each other, ask the children to count the numbers in each group, making it a **mathematics** experience.

 To incorporate **art**, ask the children to draw their assigned animals.

What Else I Did

_____

_____

_____

_____

_____

Simple Science

Art ★ Language Arts ★ Mathematics ★ Music ★ Science ★ Social Studies

Floating on Air

What It Teaches

★ An introduction to flotation

★ The movement element of force

★ The concepts of up and down

What You'll Need

Chiffon scarves (one per child) or a substitute, like paper towel squares, feathers, or bubbles

What to Do

★ Demonstrate for the children how bubbles, feathers, and/or chiffon scarves float through the air. Is the movement light or heavy? What are words they would use to describe the movement?

★ If you have scarves available for the children, hand them out and let each child explore for himself or herself how the scarves gently float back down to the ground — no matter how hard they may toss them up.

★ Challenge the children to pretend to be floating themselves. Is the movement strong or light? Are their muscles tight or loose?

How to Ensure Success

Asking questions about the movement's force — using words like *gentle* and *easy* — will help get the right idea across. Having the visual example of scarves, feathers, and/or bubbles will contribute significantly to the children's comprehension.

You may want to pretend to be a gentle breeze keeping the "scarves" (the children) adrift.

What Else You Can Do

★ Encourage the children to experiment with a variety of items at the water table to determine which float and which don't. They can then simulate the movement of both the floating and the sinking items.

More Curriculum Connectors

 Asking the children to find words to describe the movement of the floating item(s) constitutes **language arts**.

 The positional concepts of up and down fall under the headings of both **art** and **mathematics**.

What Else I Did

_____

_____

_____

_____

_____

May the Force Be with You

What It Teaches

★ An introduction to gravity

★ The concepts of up and down

What You'll Need

Beanbags (one per child)

What to Do

★ Talk to the children in simple terms about why things don't stay up in the air when you toss them there. If you'd prefer not to use the word *gravity* yet, tell them the "pull of the earth" brings the objects back down.

★ Hand out the beanbags and instruct the children to toss them gently toward the ceiling, watching as they come back down to the floor.

★ Challenge the children to each count how many seconds it takes for their beanbags to come back down (or how high they can count before the beanbag reaches the floor).

★ To make the activity more challenging, ask them to see how many times they can clap or turn around before the beanbag reaches the floor. If the children wish to try to catch their beanbags instead of letting them drop, encourage them to do so; they'll need all the practice catching they can get.

How to Ensure Success

If you don't have a very large space for this activity, instruct the children not to toss their beanbags high — because that's the only way to ensure the beanbags land somewhere near the children tossing them!

What Else You Can Do

★ Explain to the children that, just like objects, people can't stay up in the air either. Challenge them to see how high they can jump, hop, or leap into the air — and to see if they can stay up there! (Since they'll be trying with all their might, be sure they land with knees bent and heels coming all the way down to the floor.)

★   Invite the children to toss objects of varying sizes and weights into the air. Do the size and weight make any difference in how fast the objects fall?

More Curriculum Connectors

 The positional concepts of up and down are important to both **mathematics** and **art**. Counting, size, and weight are also mathematics concepts.

What Else I Did

_____

_____

_____

_____

_____

It's Electric!

What It Teaches

★ An introduction to the concept of electricity being conducted

★ Sequential movement

★ Cooperation

What You'll Need

No equipment required

What to Do

★ Ask the children for examples of things that run on electricity. Then explain that when one of those things is plugged into the wall, the electricity is "conducted" (it travels) through the plug and the cord and into the object.

★ Ask the children to form a standing circle with you and to hold hands. You then squeeze the hand of one of the children next to you, she or he squeezes the hand of the next child, and so on, all the way around the circle. Explain that, like electricity, the squeeze is traveling (being conducted) all around the circle, as though they were an electrical cord.

★ Try it again, this time adding a vibration to your body as you squeeze so they can really envision the "electricity" flowing.

How to Ensure Success

Having you as part of the circle will definitely help. However, if the children express any confusion over the idea of sequential movement, instruct one child at a time to squeeze the hand of the next child, calling them by name.

What Else You Can Do

★ Remind the children of some of the things they determined require electricity to operate. Challenge them to each choose one item and to demonstrate how it looks, moves, or functions.

More Curriculum Connectors

 Sequential is a **mathematics** concept.

 The cooperation required enhances **social studies**.

 Electricity is one of the concepts explored in Kimbo's album *Science in a Nutshell* (**music**).

What Else I Did

_____

_____

_____

_____

_____

Balancing Act

What It Teaches

★ Balance

★ Identification of center of gravity

★ Body part identification

★ Counting

What You'll Need

Mats or carpeting would be preferable to the floor

What to Do

★ Challenge the children to balance on specific body parts on the floor (mat) and to then count to five, remaining as still as they can while counting. You might include such parts as hands and feet, hands and knees, knees and elbows, feet and bottom, or hands and bottom. More challenging would be one hand and one foot, etc., and just bottom, knees, or feet on tiptoe.

★ The next step (now or at a later time) is to challenge the children to balance on a certain *number* of parts on the floor, again holding as still as possible for a count of five. (You'll be able to assess immediately which children are having difficulty counting.)

How to Ensure Success

If necessary, count aloud to five yourself, at first counting quickly and gradually lengthening the amount of time it takes to get from one to five.

When working with numbers of body parts, begin with a high number, such as five, working your way down to one (if that's feasible for your group). Be sure to ask for multiple solutions to each challenge. Encourage the children to each find at least two different ways to balance on, for example, four body parts.

Keep in mind that children don't necessarily think as we do. For them, a foot sometimes counts as one body part and sometimes as five parts. Sometimes a bottom counts as one body part and sometimes as two.

What Else You Can Do

★   Once the children are ready, explore the more difficult concept of balance and recovery with them. Ask them to balance on their knees or their seat only and lean in different directions, going as far as they can without tipping over and then returning to their original positions.

★   More challenging is the concept of counterbalance, in which partners create balances that couldn't be possible for just one person (for example, leaning against each other, back-to-back).

More Curriculum Connectors

 Counting, whether it be the number of seconds a position is held or the number of body parts, means these activities also fall under **mathematics**.

 The alternate activity focusing on counterbalance requires cooperation between partners, which links it to **social studies**.

 Add **language arts** to the mix by using David Evans and Claudette Williams' book *Make It Balance*.

What Else I Did

_____

_____

_____

_____

_____

The Machine

What It Teaches

★ An awareness of the contribution parts make to machinery as a whole

★ Cooperation

★ Practice with nonlocomotor movement

What You'll Need

No equipment needed

What to Do

★ One child begins by repeatedly performing a movement that can be executed in one spot. A second child then stands near the first and contributes a second movement that relates in some way to the first. (For example, if the first child is performing an up-down motion by bending and stretching, the second child might choose to do the reverse, standing beside her or his classmate.)

★ A third child is then added, performing a movement of his or her own. (To continue with the preceding example, the third child might choose an arm or leg motion timed to move between the two bodies bending and stretching.)

★ The movements of the first three children continue as each remaining child adds a functioning "part" to the machine.

★ Once all the parts are functioning, ask the children to each make a sound that corresponds to her or his movement.

How to Ensure Success

At first, you may find it necessary to actually suggest movement possibilities to the children.

Remind the children that they may choose any movements as long as they don't interfere with the actions of others and they contribute in some way to the machine.

What Else You Can Do

★ The six simple machines are the lever, wheel, pulley, inclined plane, screw, and wedge (Gilbert, 1977). Bring attention to some of these by asking the children to roll like wheels and twist like screwdrivers (or screws being driven in) and to demonstrate the shapes of inclines and wedges with their bodies or body parts. Levers with which the children are familiar — and which they can imitate — include scissors, wheelbarrows, and seesaws.

More Curriculum Connectors

 The cooperation required of the principal activity is a component of **social studies**.

 The production of sound, as required in the final step of the main activity, falls under the heading of **music**.

 To include **language arts**, read David Macaulay's *The Way Things Work*. Other possibilities include Michael Dahl's *Inclined Planes, Levers, Pulleys,* and *Wheels and Axles*.

What Else I Did

_____

_____

_____

_____

_____

It's Magnetic!

What It Teaches

★ Principles of magnetics

★ Cooperation

★ Directionality

What You'll Need

A set of magnets

What to Do

★ Demonstrate for the children how opposite poles attract (stick together) and identical poles repel (move away from each other). Explain that one end is called a "north" pole and the other a "south" pole.

★ Magically turn the children themselves into magnets. Ask them to move around the room as though they were magnets with only north or south poles. What happens when two such magnets (children) approach each other?

How to Ensure Success

If the idea of north and south poles is too complicated for the group, use terms like "one end" and the "other end," or anything else you deem appropriate.

Remind the children, for safety reasons, that repelling magnets never do touch one another.

What Else You Can Do

★ Assign half of the class to act as north poles and the other half as south poles (or ask them to decide themselves which they would like to be). The north poles should point a finger or hand toward the ceiling, while the south poles point toward the floor. Now what happens when two magnets get close to each other? (If two identical poles meet, they repel; if two opposite poles meet, they stick together.)

More Curriculum Connectors

 Cooperation is key to **social studies**.

 Directionality is a component of both **art** and **mathematics**.

What Else I Did

_____

_____

_____

_____

_____

SOCIAL STUDIES

Art ★ Language Arts ★ Mathematics ★ Music ★ Science ★ Social Studies

Lessons in social studies for young children begin with the children themselves — because that is where their world begins. Self-concept, therefore, is the logical starting point in the early childhood social studies curriculum. The child's world then extends, respectively, to family, friends, neighborhood, and the community in general (Mayesky, 1995; Raines & Canady, 1990).

As children learn about themselves and about each other, they discover how they are alike and different. They explore feelings, rules for living (particularly with regard to safety), holidays and celebrations, traditions and cultures, and the jobs that keep a community functioning. The following games and activities explore topics that typically come under the heading of social studies in early childhood settings: self-concept, families and friends, holidays and celebrations, occupations, and transportation.

Because being a friend or family member involves being and working together, that section consists primarily of cooperative games. The section devoted to holidays and celebrations includes activities of a "generic" nature, focusing on the spirit of holidays and celebrations rather than specific occasions. (Possibilities abound for exploring specific holidays through movement, as each offers a multitude of images. Children can move like black cats and ghosts at Halloween; Santa, elves, and reindeer at Christmas; cooks at Thanksgiving; and so on.) Under occupations, I've chosen to give children a sense of the many opportunities they have available to them in the future, regardless of gender. I've also included an activity related to the performing and visual arts so as not to exclude less "traditional" choices.

UNIT 27
Self-Concept

Art ★ Language Arts ★ Mathematics ★ Music ★ Science ★ Social Studies

"If You're Happy"

What It Teaches

★   Awareness and expression of emotions

What You'll Need

No equipment needed

What to Do

★   Teach the children the first verse of "If You're Happy," performing it the traditional way ("If you're happy and you know it, clap your hands").

★   Ask the children for suggestions of other movements to demonstrate happiness (e.g., tapping feet, waving hello, nodding the head, shouting "hooray").

★   Perform the song repeatedly, using as many of the children's suggestions as time allows.

How to Ensure Success

Ask the children to tell you about times they've been really happy. How did their faces look at the time? What movements did their hands and/or bodies perform when they felt that way?

What Else You Can Do

★   Ask the children for suggestions of other emotions they could sing about. Possibilities include feeling sad, tired, angry, or hungry. What motions and facial expressions go along with the feelings they choose? How would they sing the song if they were feeling that way? Perform the song, using as many of their suggestions as time allows.

More Curriculum Connectors

 Singing is one of the ways children experience **music**.

 Learning and creating song lyrics constitute **language arts**, as does discussing feelings of happiness and their causes. You can also make Catherine Arnholt's book *What Makes Me Happy?* part of the activity.

What Else I Did

_____

_____

_____

_____

_____

Oh, What a Feeling

What It Teaches

★   Awareness and expression of emotions

What You'll Need

No equipment needed

What to Do

★   Ask the children to demonstrate how their bodies would look if they were feeling sad, mad, tired, proud, scared, and happy.

★   Challenge them to show you how they would walk if they were feeling those same emotions.

How to Ensure Success

Talk to the children about these different emotions and times they may have experienced them. What makes them sad, mad, etc.?

What Else You Can Do

★   Ask the children to demonstrate these same emotions with just their faces, just their hands, or both together.

More Curriculum Connectors

 Asking the children to describe events that caused them to feel certain emotions constitutes **language arts**. Read Aliki's *Feelings* to the children.

 Using selections from Hap Palmer's *Ideas, Thoughts, and Feelings* brings in **music**.

What Else I Did

_____

_____

_____

_____

_____

"Punchinello"

What It Teaches

★ Self-awareness

★ Self-confidence

What You'll Need

No equipment needed

What to Do

★ Ask the children to form a circle, with one child in the center ("Punchinello").

★ The children in the circle chant, "What can you do, Punchinello, funny fellow? What can you do, Punchinello, funny you?"

★ The child in the center chooses a skill, movement, or shape to demonstrate.

★ The rest of the children then chant, "We can do it, too, Punchinello, funny fellow. We can do it, too, Punchinello, funny you." The children demonstrate the skill, movement, or shape.

How to Ensure Success

If you have children who are too shy at first to perform in the center, ask only those children who want to demonstrate to act as Punchinello.

Be sure the children realize that everyone who wants a turn will get a turn. (Be sure you leave enough time to keep that promise.)

Explain that Punchinello can demonstrate any skill, movement, or shape he or she wants to demonstrate, but that it should be something everybody else will be able to do, too.

What Else You Can Do

★ Play Pass a Face, in which the children sit in a circle and one child begins by making a face that is "passed" to the child to his right or left. That child makes the *same* face and passes it along in the same direction. When the face has been passed all around the circle, the process is repeated, with a different child beginning.

★ Play Pass a Movement, in which the children form a standing circle and pass around an *action*. The first child might, for instance, bend at the waist and straighten. Each child, in succession, must do the same.

More Curriculum Connectors

 The rhyme in the original game constitutes **language arts**.

 The sequential movement of the alternate games incorporates a **mathematics** concept.

 Being able to physically replicate what the eyes see is essential to **art**.

What Else I Did

_____

_____

_____

_____

_____

UNIT 28

Families and Friends

Art ★ Language Arts ★ Mathematics ★ Music ★ Science ★ Social Studies

This Is My Friend

What It Teaches

★ Awareness and appreciation of others

★ Sequential movement

★ An introduction to laterality

What You'll Need

No equipment needed

What to Do

★ The children stand in a circle holding hands, and one child raises the arm of the child to her right or left saying, "This is my friend. . . ." The child whose arm has been raised announces his name and then raises the arm of the next child in the circle saying, "This is my friend. . . ."

★ The process continues all the way around the circle, with arms remaining raised until the last child has had a chance to say her name. When that happens, the children take a deep bow for a job well done.

How to Ensure Success

Until the children are familiar with this game, stand in the circle with them and start the activity yourself.

If necessary, help the children with reminders of who's next, to keep arms in the air, etc.

What Else You Can Do

★ This game, adapted from Orlick (1978), is a great way for children to learn one another's names. Once they have learned them, they can introduce each other. In other words, one child raises the arm of the child to his right or left and says, "This is my friend [Kara]."

★ Play a game called Who's Missing? to create greater awareness among the children. In this game, the children sit with their eyes closed. Tap one child on the shoulder, who quietly sneaks away to a predetermined spot out of sight of the other children. When you tell the children it's all right to open their eyes, they must look around and figure out which one of them is missing!

More Curriculum Connectors

  Lifting arms *high* and moving *sequentially around the circle* qualifies This Is My Friend as an exercise in **mathematics**.

 The alternate activity relies on observational skills, which are essential to **science**.

The concept of friendship is explored in such books as James Marshall's *George and Martha One Fine Day,* Miriam Cohen's *Best Friends,* Taro Goni's *My Friends,* and Helme Heine's *Friends* (**language arts**).

What Else I Did

_____

_____

_____

_____

_____

All in the Family

What It Teaches

★   Awareness of family roles

★   Role-playing/self-expression

What You'll Need

No equipment needed

What to Do

★   Talk to the children about their families, asking how many members their families include, whether they're the oldest or youngest sibling or an only child, etc., to give the children a chance to contemplate their families and how they may be alike or different from their classmates' families.

★   Discuss the various roles different family members play in the household. For instance, the children themselves may be responsible for certain chores around the house. What are their siblings' responsibilities? Maybe Dad cooks and Mom washes dishes. Does Grandma fish or knit? Does Grandpa garden or whittle sticks?

★   One at a time, ask the children to demonstrate — through movement alone — a role played or task accomplished by either themselves or one of their family members. After a child has demonstrated, ask the rest of the children to guess what the task or role was and then to perform the movement(s) themselves.

★   Repeat until every child has a chance to demonstrate.

How to Ensure Success

If you have too large a group or if the children aren't ready to handle this challenge all at once, repeat the process only one or two times. Be sure the children realize they'll all have a turn eventually.

If the children aren't forthcoming with responses of their own, prompt them with questions like, "Who does the dishes?" or "Do you have a pet?" or "Whose job is it to feed the pet?"

What Else You Can Do

★ Talk to the children about some of the activities the adults in the family perform that they'll one day learn to do, too. Using their responses, ask them to depict some of these activities. Possibilities include driving a car, grocery shopping, or playing a sport like tennis or golf.

More Curriculum Connectors

 The discussion of family roles qualifies as a facet of **language arts**. Mercer Mayer's book *Me Too!* and Rosmarie Hausherr's *Celebrating Families* are appropriate accompaniments to these activities.

 Incorporate **music** with selections from Thomas Moore's album *The Family*.

What Else I Did

_____

_____

_____

_____

_____

Palm to Palm

What It Teaches

★ Cooperation

★ The movement element of shape

What You'll Need

No equipment needed

What to Do

★ After children choose partners, they stand facing each other, close enough to touch.

★ The first child assumes a shape with her or his arms, with palms facing those of her or his partner (for example, the first child raises both arms above the head with palms facing the second child). The partner then forms the identical shape, touching palms with those of the first child.

★ As soon as contact is made, the first child chooses a new arm position, and the activity proceeds accordingly.

★ After a while, partners reverse roles.

How to Ensure Success

Before beginning, have the children experiment with the different shapes they can make with their arms.

Once the game begins, any shape is acceptable as long as palms face the partner. If the children are unclear on this concept, physically assist them.

What Else You Can Do

★ When the children show they can successfully match palms, have them try Footsie Rolls! In this game, pairs of children lie on their backs with the soles of their feet together and then attempt to roll without their feet breaking contact. (Successful experience with logs rolls is a prerequisite.) Even if they don't get very far, children find this game hilarious.

More Curriculum Connectors

 The element of shape is vital to both **art** and **mathematics**.

What Else I Did

_____

_____

_____

_____

_____

Musical Hoops

What It Teaches

★ Cooperation

★ Practice with locomotor skills

★ Problem solving

What You'll Need

One hoop per child; any lively recording

What to Do

★ Scatter hoops throughout the room and instruct the children to each stand inside one.

★ Start playing the musical selection you've chosen, at which time the children begin to walk around the room. As the children are walking, remove one of the hoops.

★ When the music stops, the children must step inside the closest hoop, sharing the ones remaining.

★ Assign the children a different locomotor skill for the next round and begin the music again, once more removing a hoop.

★ The game continues until there is just one hoop remaining, which the children must decide how to share.

How to Ensure Success

If the children are familiar with the traditional version of Musical Chairs, reassure them no one is left out of this game, which is adapted from Hammett (1992).

Give the children a chance to problem solve on their own. If they can't figure out a way to share the dwindling number of hoops, make suggestions. One possibility is for each child to place just one foot inside a hoop.

Suggest only those locomotor skills you're sure everyone in the group can perform.

What Else You Can Do

★   Substitute chairs for the hoops, playing a game of Cooperative Musical Chairs. This is more challenging than Musical Hoops.

More Curriculum Connectors

 Music is an important part of this activity.

 The listening skills required — differentiating between sound and silence — fall not only under the heading of music but of **language arts**, too. Read Lauren Murphy Payne's *We Can Get Along* to reinforce the concept of cooperative behavior.

What Else I Did

_____

_____

_____

_____

_____

It Takes Two

What It Teaches

★ Cooperation

★ Problem solving

★ Body part identification

What You'll Need

No equipment needed

What to Do

★ Ask the children to choose partners.

★ After the children select partners, ask them to connect various body parts —
   one at a time — and see how many ways they can move without breaking the
   connection. Possible connections include right or left hands, right or left
   elbows, one or both knees, right or left feet, or backs.

How to Ensure Success

Remind the children they have two challenges: to stay connected and to discover
how many ways they can move while connected.

If necessary, make suggestions for different locomotor skills, changes in level,
changes in direction, etc. Be sure to call out all the different responses you see. Not
only is this validating for the children, but it can also provide new ideas for them.

Be sure to give the children ample time to explore all the possibilities with one connection before moving on to the next.

What Else You Can Do

★ For more of a challenge, connect *nonmatching* body parts (for example, a hand
   to an elbow, an elbow to a shoulder, or a hand to a back).

★ Play a game of Synchronized Partners, which requires pairs of children to
   cooperate *without* touching. In this game, one partner begins by repeatedly

performing a movement that can be executed in one spot. His or her partner stands near the first and performs a movement that relates in some way — without interfering — to the first. After they've had a chance to experience the "synchronicity," partners reverse roles and try again with new movements.

More Curriculum Connectors

 Matching and nonmatching (body parts) are **mathematics** concepts.

What Else I Did

_____

_____

_____

_____

_____

Holidays and Celebrations

Art ★ Language Arts ★ Mathematics ★ Music ★ Science ★ Social Studies

244

Pass the Present

What It Teaches

★ Cooperation

★ Sharing

★ The spirit of holidays and celebrations

What You'll Need

No equipment needed

What to Do

★ Talk to the children about the spirit of giving and sharing, which is what holidays and celebrations are all about.

★ With the children sitting in a circle, choose one child to begin. That child stands and depicts the movement or shape of a favorite present (or one she would like to receive).

★ The child to her right or left (depending on which direction you've chosen to move in) imitates that movement or shape and then chooses one of his own. The process continues around the circle until every child has a chance to "pass a present." (The game concludes with the first child imitating the shape or movement of the last child.)

How to Ensure Success

For maximum involvement from the children waiting their turn, ask them to guess what each present is.

What Else You Can Do

★ An alternative is to play the game in a manner similar to "Punchinello." The child whose turn it is moves to the center of the circle, then *all* of the children imitate her or his movement or shape before the next child takes a turn. (This may be preferable if you have a very large group, as it eliminates the waiting.)

More Curriculum Connectors

 Shape is a component of both **art** and **mathematics**.

 Play the appropriate holiday **music** as this game is taking place.

 To further incorporate **art**, before or after the game, ask the children to draw their favorite present.

What Else I Did

_____

_____

_____

_____

_____

Light the Candles

What It Teaches

★   Awareness of symbolism representing the holiday spirit

★   Experience with the movement elements of shape, time, force, and flow

What You'll Need

Candle and matches (optional)

What to Do

★   Talk to the children about the different times candles are used to help celebrate a holiday or special occasion. (Possibilities include birthdays, Hanukkah, and Halloween.)

★   If you have a candle available, show it to the children, talking about its shape and size and what it's made of. Is it hard or soft? Light the candle and ask the children to concentrate on the movement of the flame. What words would they use to describe it? Is it gentle or strong? If you have the time, take a few minutes to watch the candle begin to melt, discussing this process as well. Then suddenly blow it out. (You can hold this discussion without a candle; simply ask the children to recall one they've seen.)

★   Ask the children to each pretend to *be* a candle, at first made of hard wax and unlit.

★   Then pretend to light them. How would they demonstrate the flame flickering on top of them?

★   Invite them to show you how they slowly melt. After they've had a few moments to demonstrate, suddenly "blow them out." How would they show you they've been "extinguished"?

How to Ensure Success

The more words you and the children use to describe the candle and the process, the more accurately they'll be able to demonstrate. If necessary, repeat some of the words as the activity is taking place.

What Else You Can Do

★   Ask the children to make a fist (or fists), pretending their fingers are candles about to be lit. Counting aloud with you, they "light" (open) one finger at a time. When they've reached the predetermined number (for example, the number representing their age or the number 8 for the eight nights of Hanukkah), they then "extinguish" (close) one finger at a time. Once they can demonstrate this, each time you repeat the process increase the tempo at which you call out the numbers.

More Curriculum Connectors

 The concept of shape is related to both **art** and **mathematics**, the latter of which is also explored in the alternate activity.

 The concepts of fire and melting fall under the heading of **science**, as does the movement element of force.

 The discussion of candles constitutes **language arts**.

 There are several possibilities for incorporating **music**, including Steve and Greg's *Holidays and Special Times,* Jill Gallina's *Holiday Songs for All Occasions,* Tickle Tune Typhoon's *Keep the Spirit,* Hap Palmer's *Holiday Songs and Rhythms* and *Holiday Magic,* and Rae Pica and Richard Gardzina's *Moving Through the Holidays* (part of *More Music for Moving & Learning*).

What Else I Did

_____

_____

_____

_____

_____

Let's Hear It for the USA

What It Teaches

★ Awareness of patriotism and its symbols

★ The movement element of shape

What You'll Need

A United States flag or a picture of one (optional)

What to Do

★ Talk to the children about holidays celebrating various aspects of our country (e.g., Independence Day, Memorial Day, Presidents' Day, and Flag Day). Discuss the United States flag, which represents our country. Talk to them about the number of stars and stripes and the proper way to treat the flag.

★ Ask the children to demonstrate a flag being raised up a flagpole, waving proudly in the breeze, being lowered, and being folded.

★ Challenge them to show you the shape of first the stripes and then the stars.

How to Ensure Success

Encourage the children in their depictions by verbally describing each step of the process. For instance, does the flag move slowly or quickly up the flagpole? Does it move smoothly or jerkily?

If the children have a chance to watch a flag being raised at school or at a public building (or a videotape of this event), it will have more meaning for them.

What Else You Can Do

★ In the spirit of celebrating patriotism, ask the children to show you fireworks, perhaps to the accompaniment of Tchaikovsky's *1812 Overture*.

★ Hold a "parade" in the classroom or on the playground. Who and what are the various participants in a parade? Which do the children want to be? If they'd like to be in the marching band, what instruments do they want to play?

(Accompany this activity with a John Philip Sousa march or selections from Hap Palmer's *Marching*.)

More Curriculum Connectors

 The element of shape is related to both **art** and **mathematics**. The latter can further be explored by counting stars and stripes.

 Accompanying the alternative activities with the suggested compositions incorporates **music**. You can also accompany the main activity with a patriotic song, too.

 Make **language arts** and multicultural education (**social studies**) part of the experience by reading *Who Belongs Here? An American Story* by Margy Burns Knight, a book about immigration in our country (also available in Spanish).

What Else I Did

_____

_____

_____

_____

_____

Occupations

Art ★ Language Arts ★ Mathematics ★ Music ★ Science ★ Social Studies

"This Is the Way We . . ."

What It Teaches

★   Awareness of and respect for various occupations and career choices

What You'll Need

No equipment needed

What to Do

★   Talk to the children about the different jobs it takes to run a community. Ask each child, in turn, what they want to be when they grow up.

★   As each child answers your question, ask her or him to demonstrate an action performed by a person holding that job. The rest of the children then imitate the action.

★   Repeat the process until every child has a turn.

How to Ensure Success

If a child can't think of an appropriate action to go along with his or her chosen occupation, suggest several possibilities, allowing the child to choose the one she or he would like to perform.

What Else You Can Do

★   Call out an occupation, challenging the children to call out a corresponding action. Choose one at a time for the children to perform while singing "This is the way we . . ." to the tune of "The Mulberry Bush." (For example, "This is the way we paint the house" or "This is the way we slide down the pole.")

More Curriculum Connectors

 The discussion of various occupations brings **language arts** into the activity.

 The piggyback song suggested in the alternate activity involves both **language arts** and **music**.

What Else I Did

_____

_____

_____

_____

_____

Equal Opportunity

What It Teaches

★   The concept of options for all, regardless of gender

★   Appreciation for a variety of occupations

★   Role-playing

What You'll Need

No equipment needed

What to Do

★   Talk to the children about various occupations frequently associated with one gender or another, *without* mentioning gender (e.g., chefs, homemakers, hairstylists, police officers, carpenters, and dancers). Ask them to tell you some of the tasks performed by people in these occupations.

★   Challenge the children to act out some of these tasks, one at a time.

How to Ensure Success

For some occupations, you might ask the children to show you specific actions (e.g., a homemaker *washing windows* or a police officer *directing traffic*) to narrow the possibilities and avoid confusion or, as in the case of the police officer, to eliminate unwanted responses. Otherwise, simply ask them to show you, for instance, a chef or hairstylist *at work*.

To achieve the lesson's objective, be sure to encourage *all* the children, regardless of gender, to act out each occupation.

What Else You Can Do

★   Once the children have ample experience with this activity, play a game in which you call out the occupations faster and faster, in random order.

★   Play a game in which one child at a time depicts an action related to an occupation of her or his choice, with the rest of the children trying to guess the profession.

More Curriculum Connectors

 Discussion of the various roles performed by people in different occupations constitutes **language arts**. Dee Ready's *Community Helpers* series includes ten books for kindergarten to grade three focusing on the helping aspects of men and women in common careers.

What Else I Did

_____

_____

_____

_____

_____

Makin' Music

What It Teaches

★ Appreciation for an arts-related occupation

★ Role-playing

What You'll Need

Child-sized instruments (optional)

What to Do

★ Talk to the children about rock and roll bands. What instruments are typically found in them?

★ Invite the children to pretend to be in a band, playing the instruments they would like to play.

★ Challenge them to "play" each of the other instruments.

How to Ensure Success

The children think first of electric guitars and drums. Be sure to ask them about such other possibilities as keyboards, saxophone, and trumpet. Encourage them to consider the difference between playing an *acoustic* guitar and an electric one.

When the children first take part in this activity, they will probably respond by mimicking such actions as they may have seen on television or as performed by an older sibling (for example, wildly playing "air guitar"). Once they've had a chance to express themselves, gently encourage them to use as much realism in their depictions as possible. For instance, drummers have a number of different drums, as well as cymbals, to play. Keyboardists often have two or three keyboards, side by side or one above another on racks in front of them.

What Else You Can Do

★ Having started with rock and roll, which is probably the style most familiar to young children, repeat the preceding process with such musical organizations as orchestras and marching bands, which offer wider choices of instruments.

If you have child-sized instruments available, hold an actual "parade" in your classroom or around the playground.

★   At various times, when the children are involved in painting, expose them to music performed by each of these three different kinds of musical groups. You'll find, for example, that soft orchestral music results in long, flowing strokes of the paintbrush, while rock and roll causes short, staccato jabs.

★   Talk to the children about different kinds of *dancers* (e.g., ballet, tap, ballroom), challenging them to depict the actions of each.

More Curriculum Connectors

 This lesson plan is also about appreciation for **music**.

 Discussion of the various kinds of musical groups and dancers constitutes **language arts**.

 Playing music as the children are painting combines **music** and **art**.

What Else I Did

_____

_____

_____

_____

_____

Keepin' House

What It Teaches

★ Appreciation for an occupation often undervalued

★ Role-playing

What You'll Need

No equipment needed

What to Do

★ Discuss with the children some of the chores involved in keeping house. How many are they responsible for? Which ones?

★ One at a time, call out various housekeeping tasks, asking the children to show you what it looks like to perform them.

How to Ensure Success

Don't worry about realism at first; let the children pretend to their hearts' content.

Be sure to point out the differences you see in responses. For example, some children pretend to wash windows horizontally, others vertically, and still others diagonally; some pretend to use a squeegee. Let them know it's all right to find their own way.

What Else You Can Do

★ Ask the children to pretend to be housecleaning objects, for example, a vacuum cleaner, broom, feather duster, dish rag, sponge, or dishwasher.

More Curriculum Connectors

 Accompany these activities with the children's favorite cleanup song to incorporate **music**.

 Pretending to be a vacuum cleaner or dishwasher explores the concept of machinery, which falls under the heading of **science**.

What Else I Did

_____

_____

_____

_____

_____

Transportation

"Row, Row, Row Your Boat"

What It Teaches

★ Awareness of certain types of transportation

What You'll Need

Carpet squares (optional)

What to Do

★ If the children don't know the song, teach them to sing "Row, Row, Row Your Boat." If they do know it, review it. (Raffi offers a recorded version on his album *Rise and Shine*.)

★ Designate one spot in the room as the starting point and another, as far away as possible, as the finishing point.

★ Ask the children to imagine the room is a big lake and that they're going to row a boat across it. Do they know the motion involved in rowing?

★ At your signal, the children begin to row, singing "Row, Row, Row Your Boat."

★ Repeat the activity back and forth across the "lake," as long as the children remain interested.

How to Ensure Success

To offer the children variety and broaden the scope of the activity, suggest different tempos (slow, medium, and fast), pathways (straight, curving, and zigzagging), and amounts of effort (rowing lightly versus rowing strongly).

What Else You Can Do

★ If you have carpet squares available, each child can sit on one and use her or his feet to "scoot" across the lake, still making a rowing action with the arms. (This is great exercise for them!)

★ Repeat the main activity with other modes of transportation, creating the appropriate piggyback lyrics (for example, "Paddle, paddle, paddle the canoe . . .").

★   Sing and act out "The Wheels on the Bus." (This song is also on Raffi's *Rise and Shine* album.) Change the lyrics to accommodate other modes of transportation having wheels.

More Curriculum Connectors

 Since song and lyrics are very much a part of these activities, both **music** and **language arts** are involved. Flora McDonnell's *I Love Boats* is an excellent accompaniment to these activities.

What Else I Did

_____

_____

_____

_____

_____

Traffic Lights

What It Teaches

- ★   Traffic safety
- ★   Color discrimination
- ★   Motor control
- ★   The movement element of flow

What You'll Need

Three large pieces of paper: one red, one yellow, and one green; materials for an obstacle course (optional)

What to Do

- ★   Talk to the children about traffic lights and what's meant by each of the three colors.
- ★   Explain to the children that they're going to walk all around the room, pretending they're driving cars. When they see you hold up the red paper, they're to come to a complete stop. When they see you hold up yellow, they should walk in place. When you hold up green, they're to walk again.

How to Ensure Success

Make sure your "traffic lights" are big enough to be seen throughout the room. Hold them high above your head.

Present the colors in the same order for a while. Once the children are experiencing success, add to the challenge by mixing up the order.

What Else You Can Do

- ★   To enhance this game, create a "town" by decorating and/or designating certain areas of the room as various locales, for example, a gas station, the grocery store, the mall, or the library. Ask the children for suggestions. Where do their parents drive them?

★   Set up an obstacle course that includes objects the "cars" must move around, over (such as bridges), and through (such as tunnels).

★   Play the game using different locomotor skills.

More Curriculum Connectors

 The concept of color is central to **art**.

 Discussing traffic safety and the community constitutes **language arts**.

 The concepts of over, around, and through fall under the heading of **mathematics**.

What Else I Did

_____

_____

_____

_____

_____

All Aboard!

What It Teaches

★   Awareness of a form of transportation becoming less common

★   Practice with locomotor skills

★   Cooperation

What You'll Need

Masking tape or rope; hand drum and mallet (all optional)

What to Do

★   Talk to the children about trains and how they are a mode of transportation not only for people but for products. Do they realize trains are made up of individual cars linked together? Have they ever sat at a railroad crossing waiting for a train to go by and counted the number of cars in it?

★   Explain to the children that they're each going to be individual cars of a train that have been separated from one another but are still going. They're to travel about the room, moving "like trains." When they hear you say "Choo-choo," they connect with one more "car." (If desired, set an appropriate beat with a drum, stopping every time you say "Choo-choo.")

★   The game continues until all the cars are linked and the train is whole once again.

How to Ensure Success

Make sure the children understand they're to link up with whichever car is *closest* to them at the time you say "Choo-choo."

Encourage the children to walk at first as they pretend to be train cars. Once they have some experience with it, suggest alternate locomotor skills, like running or jumping.

This is one activity where sound only enhances the experience. Let them "chug" away!

What Else You Can Do

★   Use lines you may already have on the floor or create some with masking tape
or rope, asking the children to imagine the lines are narrow train tracks. Challenge the children to move along them in various ways without "falling off."
Possibilities include forward, sideward, backward, and at low and high levels.
This is a great balance activity.

More Curriculum Connectors

 Ask the children to count how many cars their completed train has (or
count the number of cars yourself, aloud) to incorporate **mathematics**.

 Balance is a concept that falls under the heading of **science**.

 Using a drum accompaniment adds an element of **music**.

 Reading David McPhail's *The Train* brings in **language arts**.

What Else I Did

_____

_____

_____

_____

_____

By Air or By Sea

What It Teaches

★ Familiarity with various modes of air and sea transportation

★ Problem solving

What You'll Need

No equipment needed

What to Do

★ Ask the children to name and depict as many modes of transportation as they can that travel in the air or on the water.

How to Ensure Success

You may choose to have all of the discussion at once, with the children brainstorming answers. Have them stand and act out the motions of each mode of transportation, one at a time, as you call them out, or you can immediately follow each idea the children have with the appropriate action(s).

What Else You Can Do

★ To continue with the problem solving, ask the children to think of and depict modes of transportation found primarily in cities (e.g., subways and taxies), that are motorless (e.g., hot air balloons and gliders), or that transport something other than people (e.g., wheelbarrows and garbage trucks).

More Curriculum Connectors

 Any discussion about transportation in which the children participate constitutes **language arts**. Book possibilities include Donald Crews' *Flying*, Anne Rockwell's *Things That Go*, and Betsy and Giulio Maestro's *Ferryboat*.

 To incorporate **mathematics**, ask the children to count the number of solutions they find to each problem.

What Else I Did

_____

_____

_____

_____

_____

References

Armstrong, T. (1993). *Seven kinds of smart*. New York: Penguin.

Bayless, K.M., & Ramsey, M.E. (1991). *Music: A way of life for the young child*. New York: Merrill.

Corso, M. (1993). Is developmentally appropriate physical education the answer to children's school readiness? *Colorado Journal of Health, Physical Education, Recreation and Dance, 19*(2), 6–7.

Docheff, D.M. (1992). *Hey, let's play!: A collection of P.E. games and activities for the classroom teacher*. Elma, WA: Dodge R Productions.

Driver, A. (1936). *Music and movement*. London: Oxford University Press.

Essa, E. (1992). *Introduction to early childhood education*. Albany, NY: Delmar.

Fauth, B. (1990). Linking the visual arts with drama, movement, and dance for the young child. In W.J. Stinson, (Ed.), *Moving and learning for the young child* (pp. 159–187). Reston, VA: American Alliance for Health, Physical Education, Recreation, and Dance.

Flaherty, G. (1992). The learning curve: Why textbook teaching doesn't work for all kids. *Teaching Today, 67*(6), 32–33, 56.

Gardner, H. (1983). *Frames of mind: The theory of multiple intelligences*. New York: Basic Books.

Gilbert, A.G. (1977). *Teaching the three Rs through movement experiences*. Minneapolis, MN: Burgess.

Haines, B.J.E., & Gerber, L.L. (1992). *Leading young children to music*. New York: Merrill.

Hammett, C.T. (1992). *Movement activities for early childhood*. Champaign, IL: Human Kinetics.

Hannaford, C. (1995). *Smart moves: Why learning is not all in your head*. Arlington, VA: Great Ocean Publishers.

Isenberg, J.P., & Jalongo, M.R. (1993). *Creative expression and play in the early childhood curriculum*. New York: Merrill.

Jaques-Dalcroze, E. (1931). *Eurhythmics, art, and education* (F. Rothwell, Trans.; C. Cox, Ed.). New York: A.S. Barnes.

Mayesky, M. (1998). *Creative activities for young children*. Albany, NY: Delmar.

McDonald, D.T., & Simons, G.M. (1989). *Musical growth and development: Birth through six*. New York: Schirmer Books.

Orlick, T. (1978). *The cooperative sports and games book: Challenge without competition*. New York: Random House.

Raines, S.C., & Canady, R.J. (1990). *The whole language kindergarten*. New York: Teachers College.

Sawyer, W.E., & Sawyer, J.C. (1993). *Integrated language arts for emerging literacy*. Albany, NY: Delmar.

Schirrmacher, R. (1998). *Art and creative development for young children*. Albany, NY: Delmar.

Taras, H.L. (1992). Physical activity of young children in relation to physical and mental health. In C.M. Hendricks, (Ed.), *Young children on the grow: Health, activity, and education in the preschool setting* (pp. 33–42). Washington, DC: ERIC Clearinghouse.

Werner, P.H., & Burton, E.C. (1979). *Learning through movement*. St. Louis, MO: Mosby.

Resources

Professional Organizations and Publications

★ American Alliance for Health, Physical Education, Recreation, and Dance (AAHPERD)
1900 Association Drive
Reston, VA 20191
Journal: *Journal of Physical Education, Recreation, and Dance*
Associations under AAHPERD umbrella include: National Association for Sport and Physical Education (NASPE) and National Dance Association (NDA)

★ Association for Childhood Education International (ACEI)
17904 Georgia Avenue, Suite 215
Olney, MD 20832
Journal: *Childhood Education*

★ Early Childhood Music Association (ECMA)
2110 27th Avenue
Greeley, CO 80631
Journal: *Early Childhood Connections: The Journal of Music- and Movement-Based Learning*

★ Music Educators National Conference (MENC)
1902 Association Drive
Reston, VA 20191
Journal: *Music Educators Journal*

★ National Association for the Education of Young Children (NAEYC)
1509 16th Street, NW
Washington, DC 20036
Journal: *Young Children*

Relevant Publications

★ *Dance Teacher Now*
3101 Poplarwood Court, Suite 310
Raleigh, NC 27604

★ *Moving & Learning in Early Childhood: The Movement Education Newsletter*
346 North Barnstead Road
Center Barnstead, NH 03225

★ *Teaching Elementary Physical Education*
P.O. Box 5076
Champaign, IL 61825

Movement and Physical Education Book Publishers

★ AAHPERD
1900 Association Drive
Reston, VA 20191
800/321-0789

★ Gerstung Publications
6308 Blair Hill Lane
Baltimore, MD 21209
800/922-3575

★ High/Scope
600 North River Street
Ypsilanti, MI 48198
800/407-7377

★ Human Kinetics
P.O. Box 5076
Champaign, IL 61825
800/747-4457

Sources for Ordering Recordings

★ Educational Activities, Inc.
P.O. Box 87
Baldwin, NY 11510
800/645-3739

★ Educational Record Center
3233 Burnt Mill Drive, Suite 100
Wilmington, NC 28403
800/438-1637

★ High/Scope
600 North River Street
Ypsilanti, MI 48198
313/407-7377

★ Kimbo Educational
Dept. T, P.O. Box 477
Long Branch, NJ 07740
800/631-2187

★ Melody House
819 NW 92nd Street
Oklahoma City, OK 73114
800/234-9228

★ Moving & Learning
346 North Barnstead Road
Center Barnstead, NH 03225
603/776-7411

★ Music for Little People
P.O. Box 1460
Redway, CA 95560
800/727-2233

Sources for Ordering Equipment and Props

★ Bell (Early Childhood Division)
P.O. Box 886
East Troy, WI 53120
800/543-1458

★ Childcraft
P.O. Box 3081
Edison, NJ 08818
800/631-5652

★ Chime Time
One Sportime Way
Atlanta, GA 30340
800/677-5075

★ Constructive Playthings
1227 East 119th Street
Grandview, MO 64030
800/448-1412

★ Flaghouse
601 Flaghouse Drive
Hasbrouck Heights, NJ 07604
800/793-7900

★ Gerstung
1400 Coppermine Terrace
Baltimore, MD 21209
800/922-3575

★ J.L. Hammett Co.
P.O. Box 9057
Braintree, MA 02184
800/333-4600

★ Kaplan
P.O. Box 609
Lewisville, NC 27023
800/334-2014

★ Lakeshore
2695 East Dominguez Street
Carson, CA 90749
800/428-4414

Movement Specialists and Workshops

★ Nancy Conkle
15214 Faubion Trail
Leander, TX 78641
512/259-5125
Terrific Me workshops address the movement needs of children while extolling movement as a medium for teaching any material in the curriculum.

★ Marjorie Corso
INSIGHTS
1933 County Road 782
Woodland Park, CO 80863
719/687-0963
A series of educational videos on the developmental motor skills of 2- to 7-year-old children.

★ Carol Hammett
61295 Victory Loop
Bend, OR 97702
503/382-9357
Workshops and seminars on developmentally appropriate physical education curriculum for infants, toddlers, and 3- to 5-year-old children.

★ Maureen Oosten
Kids on the Move
24 Fairway Drive
Kennebunk, ME 04043
207/967-2339
Movement education classes for 2- to 12-year-old children and consulting services, workshops, motor assessment screening, and adapted physical education services.

★ Rae Pica
Moving & Learning
346 North Barnstead Road
Center Barnstead, NH 03225
603/776-7411
e-mail: raepica//www.worldpath.net/~raepica

★ Janet E. Santopietro
P.E. For Preschools
6592 Benton Circle
Arvada, CO 80003
303/432-2234
Programs designed for children ages 2½ through kindergarten in the preschool setting. Programs focus on fundamental motor skills and related concepts in creative movement, rhythms, simple games, and use of large and small apparatus/equipment.

★ Phyllis Weikart
High/Scope
600 North River Street
Ypsilanti, MI 48198
313/485-2000, ext. 211
Offers a variety of training options as well as a Summer Institute program. Workshops include "Teaching Movement—The Young Child," "Teaching Movement—K–6 Approach," and "Teaching Movement—The Older Child."

Index

Art, 1
Color, 23
    Color Me . . ., 26
    Primary Colors, 28
    What Am I?, 24
Line, 16
    Drop Me a Line, 21
    Up and Down, Side to Side,
      and Corner to Corner, 19
    What's My Line?, 17
Shape and Size, 9
    I Spy . . ., 12
    Mirror, Mirror, 10
    Show Me . . ., 14
Spatial Relationships, 2
    Follow the Leader, 7
    Personal Space, 3
    You Can Take It With You!, 5
Texture, 30
    Feathers and Seashells and Bears,
      Oh My, 35
    Smooth and Rough, 33
    Soft and Hard, 31

Language Arts, 37
Listening, 38
    Get Into Action, 41
    How Many Sounds?, 43
    Listen Up!, 39
    What's That Sound?, 45
Reading, 54
    Action!, 55
    Descriptive Words, 57
    Happy Endings, 59
Speaking, 47
    Four Voices, 52
    Tell Me About . . ., 50
    What's in a Name?, 48

Writing, 61
    Left to Right, 62
    Show Me the Letter . . ., 64
    Skywriting, 66

Mathematics, 69
Basic Geometry, 96
    Line 'Em Up, 97
    On the Right Path, 99
    Right to the Point, 101
    What a Square!, 103
Counting, 89
    Blast Off!, 90
    How Many Parts?, 92
    Oh, the Possibilities, 94
Number Awareness and Recognition, 82
    Invisible Numbers, 87
    Number Shapes I, 83
    Number Shapes II, 85
Quantitative and Positional Concepts, 71
    Light and Heavy, 74
    The Long and the Short of It, 72
    Me and My Shadow, 78
    One More Time, 76
    Over the River and Through the Woods, 80
Simple Computation, 105
    Add 'Em and Subtract 'Em, 109
    How Many Parts Now?, 111
    "Roll Over", 106

Music, 113
Mood, 144
    In a Mellow Mood, 145
    In the Mood, 149
    What Mood Are You In?, 147

Pitch, 137
    Do-Re-Mi, 138
    High and Low, 140
    Moving High/Moving Low, 142
Rhythm, 151
    Body Rhythm, 152
    Common Meters, 158
    Echo, 156
    Match the Movement, 154
Staccato and Legato, 130
    Bound and Free, 135
    "Pop Goes the Weasel", 131
    Statues, 133
Tempo, 116
    Moving Slow/Moving Fast, 117
    Moving Slow/Moving Fast — Again, 119
    Slow to Fast and Back Again, 121
Volume, 123
    Moving Softly/Moving Loudly, 124
    Moving Softly/Moving Loudly —
      Again, 126
    Soft to Loud and Back Again, 128

Science, 161
    Animals, 200
      Creepy-Crawly, 207
      Ducks, Cows, Cats, and Dogs, 209
      Giddy-Up, 205
      My Favorite Animal, 201
      Rabbits and 'Roos, 203
    Hygiene, 173
      A Bite Out of Life, 178
      Hair Care, 176
      Laundry Day, 180
      Rub-a-Dub-Dub, 174
    My Body, 162
      A Breath of Fresh Air, 171
      Common Senses, 169
      Hands Down, 165
      Move It!, 167
      Simon Says, 163
    Nutrition, 182
      Bread, Bread, Bread, 187
      Eat Your Fruits and Veggies, 183
      Get Ready, Spaghetti!, 185
      The Great Pyramid, 189

Seasons, 191
    Autumn, 192
    Spring, 196
    Summer, 198
    Winter, 194
Simple Science, 211
    Balancing Act, 218
    Floating on Air, 212
    It's Electric!, 216
    It's Magnetic!, 222
    The Machine, 220
    May the Force Be with You, 214

Social Studies, 225
    Families and Friends, 233
      All in the Family, 236
      It Takes Two, 242
      Musical Hoops, 240
      Palm to Palm, 238
      This Is My Friend, 234
    Holidays and Celebrations, 244
      Let's Hear It for the USA, 249
      Light the Candles, 247
      Pass the Present, 245
    Occupations, 251
      Equal Opportunity, 254
      Keepin' House, 258
      Makin' Music, 256
      "This Is the Way We . . .", 252
    Self-Concept, 226
      "If You're Happy", 227
      Oh, What a Feeling, 229
      "Punchinello", 231
    Transportation, 260
      All Aboard!, 265
      By Air or By Sea, 267
      "Row, Row, Row Your Boat", 261
      Traffic Lights, 263

References, 269

Resources, 270